SHOOTING FLYING

S Gribelin Sculp.

Antique Guns and
Gun Collecting

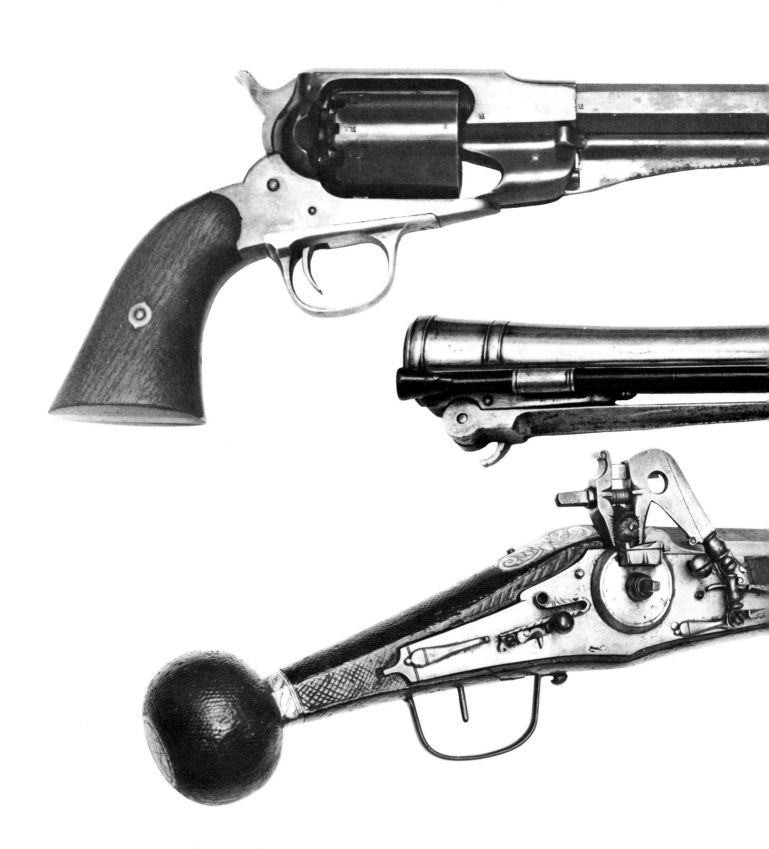

Antique Guns and

Gun Collecting

Frederick Wilkinson

CHARTWELL
BOOKS, INC.

1 *half-title page*
See plate 20.

2 *title pages*
See plates 85, 52 and 7.

Endpaper illustrations
Taken from *The Gentleman's Recreation,* London, 1709.
Front: *Stalking* and *Shooting Flying.* Back: *Pearching
the Pheasant* and *A Keeper choseing out of the Heard
a fatt Buck to be Shot and run downe.*

First published in 1974 by
The Hamlyn Publishing Group Limited
a division of the Octopus Publishing Group,
Michelin House, 81 Fulham Road, London SW3 6RB

This 1990 edition published by
CHARTWELL BOOKS, INC.
A Division of BOOK SALES, INC.
110 Enterprise Avenue, Secaucus, New Jersey 07094

ISBN 1-55521-610-2

Produced by Mandarin Offset
Printed in Hong Kong

Contents

Why and how to collect

Interest in firearms as collectors' pieces is no new fad, for they have been collected almost from the time that they were first invented in the 14th century. New collectors join a distinguished company which has included kings and emperors among its ranks. The Emperor Maximilian maintained a large armoury, and an illustrated list of the weapons survives. Louis XIII of France (reigned 1610–1643) gathered together a prime selection known today as the Cabinet d'Armes, and not only has the inventory survived but so have many of the weapons. In England the Prince Regent (1762–1830), later to become George IV (reigned 1820–1830), purchased a number of fine weapons which figure on the inventory of Carlton House. However, it must be admitted that prior to the 19th century it was very much a minority pastime; weapons were regarded by most people simply as tools, and it was not until later in the century that a more academic approach began to develop. There was a romantic interest in the Middle Ages, helped by the novels of Sir Walter Scott; swords and armour became popular, and some of this interest was channelled into the collecting of firearms. One of the finest private collections was that built up by the Marquess of Hertford and his son Sir Richard Wallace in the 19th century, and today the Wallace Collection in London houses some of the finest examples of the gunmaker's art from the 16th to the 19th centuries.

Collecting was still very limited until early this century when Major H. B. C. Pollard published, in 1926, his book *A History of Firearms*. Although much of the material is now inaccurate and many of his conclusions were based on insufficient or wrong information, this does not disgrace the author, for he was one of the first to explore the whole history of firearms and encourage their collection. Today original editions of this and other books by Pollard are much sought after. In 1938 another standard work *English Pistols and Revolvers* by J. N. George was published, and this corrected some errors and went into more detail. In 1942 George was killed in action in North Africa, and his second book, *English Guns and Rifles*, was completed by S. B. Haw and published in 1947. Both are still very readable and offer a good general grounding in the study of antique firearms. The information in them is still largely relevant, and the illustrations of George's collection have proved

invaluable for later students. In the same year there also appeared a small booklet by James Frith entitled *Pistols, Their History and Development*, which gave some advice on collecting, and today this paperback is prized by collectors.

During World War II, from 1942 onwards, England suffered an invasion which was peaceful and welcome, for into this country flooded a large number of Americans. Perhaps because of their long frontier tradition and the Civil War of 1861–1865, the Americans have always been interested in firearms. For many of them one of the first calls in this country was to the antique shops, and they found, to their delight, that there was a plentiful supply of antique firearms. They bore off their treasures with joy, the increasing demand stimulated the dealers to look further afield and seek fresh stock, and so began the spiralling of interest which continues today. Following 1945 there came the demobilisation of millions of men who had served in the war and, as a result, had more than a nodding acquaintance with firearms. Some interest remained, many began to collect, and gradually this growth of interest percolated through the antique trade. The number of auctions dealing with arms and armour increased, and publishers of books on antiques realised the potential market. In 1961 H. Blackmore's *British Military Firearms* was published, and this book remains today a classic, with its carefully documented identification of weapons of various patterns.

Greater demand resulted in higher prices, which in turn created a bigger demand for knowledge. More books appeared, and this greater flow of knowledge only increased the demand, so that the price of firearms has now reached quite startling levels.

What, then, is it that arouses such interest in these lethal weapons? First of all, it must be stressed that for the great majority of collectors the purpose of the weapon is of very minor importance. Many say that this is an escapist approach, as indeed it probably is, but very few collectors see these items as being intended to maim or kill. They are viewed purely, almost exclusively, as artistic objects in their own right; they are valued for their mechanical design and for their aesthetic appeal. Interest in a firearm may be aroused by many things, but most of the collectors, if they are honest, would admit that there is in them an element of romance. A

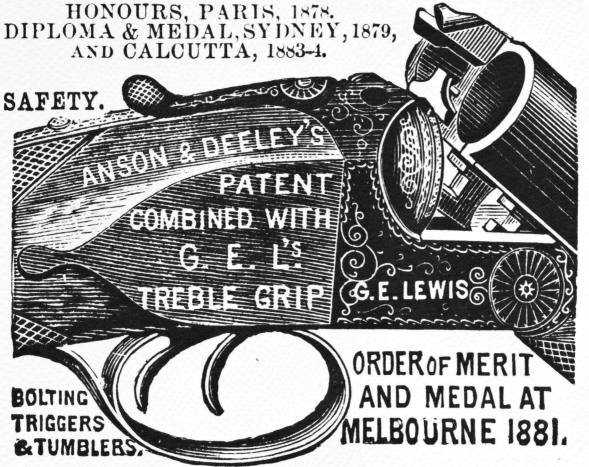

NEW CATALOGUE READY JANUARY, 1887.

"THE GUN OF THE PERIOD."
TRADE MARK.   REGD.

HONOURS, PARIS, 1878.
DIPLOMA & MEDAL, SYDNEY, 1879,
AND CALCUTTA, 1883-4.

SAFETY.

ANSON & DEELEY'S PATENT COMBINED WITH G. E. L'S TREBLE GRIP

G. E. LEWIS

BOLTING TRIGGERS & TUMBLERS.

ORDER OF MERIT AND MEDAL AT MELBOURNE 1881.

With intercepting Safety Bolt, rendering an accidental discharge impossible.

G. E. LEWIS'S TREBLE GRIP, combined with Anson and Deeley's Locking, Cocking, and Automatic Safety Bolt, is the most perfect weapon ever placed in the hands of the sportsman. The opening of this gun cocks it, and bolts the triggers and tumblers automatically. Prices from 20 to 40 guineas. A special plain quality, £16. Express Rifles, from 12 guineas. "The Gun of the Period," wherever shown, has always taken honours. Why buy from Dealers when you can buy it at half the price from the Maker? Any gun sent on approval on receipt of P.O.O., and remittance returned if, on receipt, it is not satisfactory. Target trial allowed. A choice of 2000 guns, rifles, and revolvers, embracing every novelty in the trade.—G. E. LEWIS, Gun Maker, 32 and 33, Lower Loveday-street, Birmingham. Estab. 1850.

Licence to carry and have Arms in a Proclaimed District.

No. _95_

I, _Gerard Barry_ having been duly appointed in that behalf, under an Act passed in the Eleventh Year of the Reign of Her Majesty Queen VICTORIA, intituled, "An Act for the better " prevention of Crime and Outrage in certain parts of Ireland, until the " First day of December, One Thousand Eight Hundred and Forty-nine, " and to the end of the then next Session of Parliament," do hereby grant

to _William Brell Esquire_

of _Gorey_

a Licence to carry and have

within the _County of Wexford_

One Double Gun
Four Pistols
One Sword —

Dated this _10th_ day of _August_ 184 _8_

Gerard Barry RM { Signature of Licencor.

By Authority—ALEX. THOM, 87, Abbey-street, Dublin.

flintlock pistol may never have left the workshop where it was made, but it could equally well have travelled across America with Lewis and Clarke or have seen action on the battlefield of Waterloo; it may have been used to hold up or defend a coach, or any one of a dozen or more exciting events may have befallen it.

There is, too, the uniqueness of the weapon, for prior to the introduction of mechanisation in the second quarter of the 19th century each firearm was handmade and was the result of the efforts, the care and the skill of a number of top-grade craftsmen. No two pistols were ever quite the same; even the cheapest variety had minute differences, whilst pistols supplied in pairs will, on close examination, reveal variations in detail.

There is also the general aesthetic delight: most firearms are finely made and essentially functional in shape, for the design was the outcome of hundreds of years of experimentation by craftsmen, soldiers, hunters, duellists, all trying to produce an object which would fulfil its function efficiently. The graceful curve of the butt, the balance of the weapon, are usually a joy. To our ancestors functionalism alone was not sufficient; a weapon needed to be more than dependable – it had to be attractive. The fittings of pistols and 'long arms' were chiselled, engraved, gilded, painted, blued, enamelled or decorated with any combination of these methods. Silver and other precious metals, coral and even jewels were used to decorate the pistol. Tastes vary, and some of the later examples of the mid 19th century are florid to an extreme but are, nevertheless, still of interest.

On a more practical level there is a mechanical appeal, for every firearm needs a device which will, by some means or other, ignite a charge of explosive to discharge a missile. The methods used to effect this simple basic job were numerous and varied, with many interesting details and refinements. There were safety devices to be incorporated and improvements to increase the efficiency, and there was the lunatic fringe which produced ingenious ideas that looked attractive on paper but, when translated into practical weapons, often turned out to be devices which were more dangerous to the user than to the target.

Collecting is not limited to the firearms themselves for each weapon required a number of associated items. There were flasks to hold the powder which were attractive in their own right, indeed so much so that today reproductions are being made. There were the moulds to cast the bullets, often cleverly contrived to produce a series of bullets of different sizes. There were the holsters or belts in which they might be carried either on the saddle or on oneself. Later came cased sets which contained, perhaps, a choice of barrels and a variety of loading tools often most ingeniously designed, which enabled the hunter or the duellist to strip, repair or clean the weapon.

In addition to these aesthetic and essentially intellectual attractions it must be said that there is a strong financial motivation. Whilst it is true to say that every antique has appreciated in value, antique firearms have increased far more than most; items purchased for £20 or US $50 some ten years ago are probably worth well in excess of £120 or US $300. Whilst this is gratifying to the owner of items purchased many years ago, it must be admitted that this increase has not always been to the advantage of collectors. The greatly increased percentage return has attracted the investment buyers, people who are not primarily concerned in the item itself, but merely see it as an object of merchandise. They are concerned with buying and storing it, allowing it to appreciate and then realising the asset at some later date. The intrusion of these people into the market and a greater general demand have driven up the prices of some specimens so much that today certain items are outside the province of the average collector.

Many will, no doubt, now feel that the collecting of firearms is far too expensive a field for them; but if there is a genuine interest then there are still opportunities to indulge this interest both practically as a collector and also as a student. The broad outlines of the history of firearms are known in some detail, but there are specialised fields in which much research still remains to be done. Provincial gunmakers can often be traced by research into local rate books and directories; the collecting of contemporary references to the use and construction of firearms is fascinating. Trade labels, firearms in portraits and many other similar studies all offer opportunities to the enthusiast to develop his own knowledge as well as that of others.

How to collect

The preceding section may perhaps have been a case of bringing coals to Newcastle since the reader of this volume is probably already at least partially convinced

of the virtues and benefits of a study of firearms. But now to consider the practical problems; if there is an interest how does one indulge it?

A large number of collectors would probably agree that they share a common experience in that their interest was aroused by the acquisition of the very first piece. Often it was a relic handed on by some doting aunt or aged grandparent or an old decorative piece previously cherished by no one. Unfortunately these days have long since passed, and firearms amnesties and the rising prices have rendered the chance of being presented with an antique firearm, as a gift, very remote indeed. Where then to begin? Probably the best advice that can be given is that of Mr Punch to those about to get married – don't! In this case a proviso may be added to make it read – don't before you are ready. The apparent truism cannot be too strongly emphasised. The price of mistakes in collecting is now too great to indulge oneself in this luxury too often. Knowledge is power – again a cliché, but very true. Before any serious effort is made to collect weapons it is imperative to have some broad understanding of the value, construction and general qualities of antique firearms.

Modern advances in museum display technique have led, in many cases, to the reduction of the number of items on view. If there is a local museum with one or two weapons on show, then it is well worth approaching the curator. Ask permission to view any others held in store, for it is surprising how many museums have a number of treasures tucked away in their cellars and vaults. Try to persuade the curator or director to let you see these and, of far greater importance, to handle them. There comes to every collector in whatever field he specialises, the ability to tell a great deal by the 'feel' of a thing, and this is especially true of antique firearms. There is something about the balance, the feel of the wood, the texture of the metal, which always helps in assessing the genuineness and antiquity of any particular piece. This ability to feel is a quality which varies from person to person; but it needs developing, and this can only be done by experience. There are a number of societies of collectors, and there are several publications which will occasionally give the addresses of such groups. The vast majority of collectors are only too happy to pass on their expertise and knowledge to a beginner, and most will admit to much pleasure in showing their various items and discussing them with a fellow enthusiast. If contact can be made with these groups and the interest shown is seen to be genuine, then there will be people anxious to help the beginner.

If, unfortunately, there are no possibilities of handling a variety of guns, then frequent visits to museums are even more important. It is amazing how much one can look at a thing and yet not really see it, not really notice the details. Specimens should be closely examined and studied from every angle to try and see it not only as a whole but also as a number of separate units which join together to form a whole. Examine the barrel, the wooden stock and the attached fittings and see how they are fashioned and how secured. A word of caution is necessary here: although there has been a marked improvement in general standards, not all museums have either the time, the resources or the expertise to check and correctly identify every single item in their collection. It is a common experience that in non-specialist museums weapons are one of the least well served in this respect and may often be wrongly dated or labelled. This may be the result of using out-of-date textbooks, which have long since been superseded, for the supply of authoritative literature on the subject is now quite extensive. In 1951 Ray Riling issued *Guns and Shooting,* a bibliography which listed some 2,747 titles, and in the period since that book was published the number has possibly doubled. There are a few fields which have been left unexplored but most aspects and types of antique firearms can be read about in some considerable detail. A list of reliable publications can be found in the Bibliography on page 93.

After a period of study, reading and handling, one feels that now, as the result will not be too catastrophic, it is time for the first item in the collection to be acquired. Where to find it? The obvious places are, of course, the antique shops, but here some caution is recommended. There are some antique dealers who specialise in antique firearms, but to the majority of dealers they are simply one of a whole range of antiques. The owner of a shop may be an expert in one particular type of antique, but it does not follow that he is able to value or appraise antique firearms. Fortunately his general expertise will often prevent him from making too many disastrous buys, but it has been known for general dealers to make mistakes. Bearing this fact in mind, a dealer who has some antique firearms has been found; now comes the inevitable question of price. With the non-specialist dealer both hope and despair can be present; as their knowledge is probably only sketchy it is possible for them to miss some finer details, some nice point of difference that makes one particular piece unique and worth far more than the ordinary run of items. In such cases the price they quote may well be below the item's market value. Alternatively their lack of knowledge may lead them to believe that any firearm is worth considerably more than, in fact, it will fetch on the open market. They may have heard of a similar item fetching a high price and feel that theirs too is worth just as much, but this is not necessarily the case. Specialist dealers are usually far more consistent, for they know their market and can assess a piece for what it really is. They are also better qualified to advise as to the genuineness of an item, and if they are jealous of their reputation, as they should be, then they will be honest and direct. They should also be prepared, if asked, to give some written proof as to their opinion, and failure to do so may well be cause for hesitation on the part of the purchaser. Equally well it must be remembered that often a matter may be one of opinion and that no one is infallible: even experts have been known to differ. If the collector finds a good reliable dealer, then it is well to stick with him, for he can be of enormous help with his advice.

How, then, does one assess the value of any particular piece? There is no real answer to this question, and in general it must be said that each item is worth precisely what the buyer is prepared to pay for it. One collector may value something at £500, another at not more than £30; but even so there are guidelines for assessing the average value of a particular item.

The most useful, but not necessarily the final, guide on values must be the prices fetched at public auctions. However, it will be appreciated that there is a certain artificiality about auctions: gathered together in one room are a number of determined dealers and collectors, and for any one item there may be ten potential buyers. A piece at auction may well realise a figure in excess of that which it would fetch in an ordinary market. If there are several dealers or collectors after one piece its price may be pushed up beyond its normal value. Most of the auction houses issue catalogues and price lists, and in the case of the larger houses these catalogues are often well illustrated and have full and informative descriptions. A study of these catalogues and price lists will always be extremely useful, but it must be borne in mind that catalogue descriptions are very much the opinions of the auction house: their expert is usually well qualified

but he may, consciously or unconsciously, give to the item an importance it does not possess. His understanding of the term 'good condition' may not be the same as that of another dealer or collector. It is, therefore, important to be able to assess the relative worth of the catalogue description, but in many cases this is virtually impossible since often the collector cannot visit the rooms. Possibly the best hope for the collector who is unable to view items to be auctioned is to employ the services of a commission buyer. There are a number of dealers who will undertake to bid for and, far more important, assess any lot in an auction on the instructions of a client. They will examine the item, give their assessment of the value and advise the client as to the figure he must expect to pay for it. Naturally for this service they will make a charge, which varies but is normally about 10% of the purchase price. This is usually money well spent, particularly if one finds a reliable commission agent. When using an agent it is very important to give precise instructions as to the figure to which he may go, and having once made the decision one should stick to it. It is usually a mistake to believe that 'just one more bid' will be successful, for that 'one more' is almost invariably followed by

another, and there can be an escalation well past the original figure. Here again the services of a commission buyer can be useful, for he is able to make a more detached assessment of value.

Some of the most successful collectors and dealers are those who have the quality of persistence. They visit every auction room, no matter what is being sold; they visit every secondhand furniture shop, every back street junk dealer and every antique shop they pass. Many also advertise in local newspapers, in magazines and on newsagents' notice boards, and there is no question but that all these systems will bring some successes. Any gathering of collectors will produce a crop of stories about the bargain found in such circumstances. Certainly it is well worth while cultivating every dealer, for they generally have greater opportunities for finding pieces than the average collector.

Street markets are worth a visit: the opportunities for finding a bargain, though small, are nonetheless just big enough to make it worth while paying regular calls. The best known ones are, of course, regularly swept by local dealers, and this happens very early in the morning; but odd items are brought along for sale during the day and the collector may just be lucky.

11

History of Firearms

The history of firearms really began when man threw his first stone, for the gun is a logical and inevitable extension of the earliest projectiles. Guns are designed to eject a missile at speed and in a specified direction, something which the bow did for many thousands of years. The earliest bows can be traced back to the Stone Age, when they appear in wall paintings, and with changes in design and improvements in elasticity they continued in use until the 17th century. There were two main forms of bow, the long bow and the crossbow, and the Chinese were familiar with both; indeed they designed a repeating crossbow, and it is in China that the story of firearms begins.

At an indeterminate date, probably around the 11th century, Chinese technologists experimented with combinations of various chemicals, and one they stumbled upon was a mixture of sulphur, saltpetre and charcoal—black powder or gunpowder. They did not at first realise its potential, and their main use for it was simply as a means of producing a loud noise: in fact it was a form of psychological warfare. By the 13th century they had discovered its propellant powers and were using strengthened tubes of bamboo loaded with gunpowder to fire, no doubt very inaccurately, a bullet, probably made of stone or baked clay. From this simple and crude beginning was to develop the firearm.

When the knowledge of gunpower reached Europe is uncertain, but it seems likely that its formula was known, and at least partially understood, in Europe by the 13th century. The general concensus of informed opinion is that Roger Bacon (1214–1294) was familiar with its composition. However, the first positive references to firearms do not appear until the 14th century, and the earliest references so far traced occur in the 1320s. Certainly by the middle of the 14th century it may reasonably be assumed that the use of firearms was well established, for contemporary references abound.

These early firearms were by any standards extremely crude; they seem generally to have been in the form of artillery and comprised barrels cast or fashioned from a series of laths laid upon a cylindrical former and then locked into place by a series of hoops. The design was adapted to form hand guns; these were simply smaller versions of the cannon, but unlike the artillery they were muzzle-loading. Powder and ball were placed in the breech from the open or muzzle end and were fired by touching the tip of a burning match or glowing ember to the powder in the breech by way of a small hole drilled through the top of the barrel. These hand guns were at first secured to a wooden pole or cast as part of a metal bar. In general they were used primarily for defence, and many have a hook projecting beneath the barrel so that they could be rested upon the top of a wall to be fired. Once the basic idea had been grasped it was developed, and these hand guns were given longer barrels and also made slightly more sophisticated by being secured to a wooden body known as the stock. One simple, but basically most important, invention was that of the match: a piece of cord soaked in a strong solution of potassium nitrate and then allowed to dry. Once lit, the end smouldered at the rate of about one inch per minute, so that now, equipped with a length of match, the shooter had an immediately available means of ignition. In the 15th century the serpentine was introduced: this was an S-shaped lever (hence the name) which was secured to the side of the wooden stock. It was so designed that pressure on the lower end forced the upper section to swing forward and down. The match was secured in this upper jaw just above the touch hole. During the next century the stock was gradually modified until it had acquired basically the shape of a modern long arm with a butt which could be held against the shoulder to afford the means of some sort of aim.

The matchlock, as it was now called, was to remain in use until the mid 17th century, for it was cheap to produce, simple to maintain, wildly inaccurate but, under battle conditions, reasonably effective. A hundred men or so, each with a matchlock, had only to point them in the general direction of an enemy and a certain percentage of hits would inevitably be scored. However, the matchlock was under several limitations; for instance, it was difficult, though not impossible, to cope with it on horseback. It could be, and was, done by Indian troops in the 19th century, but it was by no means easy. The match was consumed at the rate of about one inch per minute, which meant that when action was expected and the match had to be kept constantly glowing, it was essential to have fresh supplies immediately to hand. There was, of course, a very serious danger of accidental explosion, for the presence of an unprotected glowing end near quantities of powder represented an explosive situation, and accidents were not uncommon. Loading and handling a matchlock called for a complicated sequence of events, and the musketeer had to carry out some twenty different movements. The muskets were very heavy, and the long barrel had to be supported, for which purpose the musketeer used a rest consisting of a pole with a U-shaped metal arm at the top. The matchlock served its purpose well, but because of its limitations it was obviously desirable that other means of ignition should be produced.

Early in the 16th century an entirely new principle had been evolved in which ignition was by mechanical means instead of combustion. It operated by producing a shower of sparks by friction between a piece of mineral and a piece of steel. The mineral, known as pyrites, is widely distributed over the whole of Europe and was thus readily available. The mechanism consisted of a small-diameter thick steel wheel, the edge of which was grooved and cross-cut rather like a file. This wheel was made to rotate, and the pyrites was pressed against the rotating edge so that the friction between the two produced a shower of sparks. The apparatus was similar to the one used in the modern cigarette lighter. This system, known as the wheellock, remained in general use throughout the whole of the 16th century and, indeed, in parts of Europe right through the 17th. The most common arrangement consisted of a metal plate, the lockplate, to which was attached the wheel, the axle of which passed through a hole to the outside of the lockplate. This projecting lug had the end squared so that it could be engaged and rotated by means of a key. The wheel was connected by way of a short linked chain to a heavy V-shaped mainspring. If a key, known as the spanner, was placed over the end of the shank, the wheel could be rotated and pressure applied, via the chain, to the V-spring. A small spring-operated arm, the sear, was made to engage with a small recess on the side of the wheel; thus as the wheel was spanned or rotated, it was locked into place by the sear. The wheel was positioned so that its rim formed the floor of the pan situated by the touch hole which was now drilled through the side of the barrel. A small pinch of fine-grain powder, the priming, was now placed in this pan, covering the touch hole. This priming was protected from the elements by means of a sliding lid, the pan cover. The piece of pyrites was held within the adjustable jaws of a pivoted arm known as the doghead or cock. This arm could be swung clear of the pan so that a loaded weapon could be carried with perfect safety since the pyrites was not in contact with the wheel and, consequently, no sparks could be struck.

The sequence of operation was basically the same as for the matchlock but with one important difference. Powder was poured down into the breech, and seated above this was a lead ball. The wheel was spanned, that is placed under pressure, a pinch of powder was placed on to the pan and the pan cover closed. Once loaded and spanned, the weapon could be left with perfect safety and confidence for any length of time, and when it was required only two actions were needed: to swing the doghead or cock forward so that the pyrites pressed down on the pan cover and then to press the trigger. The small arm, the sear, was thus disengaged from the locking hole in the side of the wheel which was immediately forced by the mainspring to rotate quickly; at the same time the pan cover was automatically pushed clear. This allowed the arm to push down the pyrites to press against the rotating edge of the wheel. Sparks were produced and ignited the priming, and the flame or flash passed through the touch hole into the breech and so to the main charge which exploded and ejected the bullet.

The wheellock was a far-reaching innovation; it could be produced in any size, and it was thus, for the first time, perfectly possible to make firearms small enough to be carried in the pocket or attached to the belt; the pistol had arrived. The name 'pistol' is usually taken to derive from the town of Pistoia in Italy where these weapons first became popular.

The wheellock was used on many weapons: it was fitted to long arms, to pistols and to swords, maces and even crossbows so that these were, in effect, two weapons combined into one. The two main centres of production were Italy and Germany, although wheellocks were known to have been produced in France, Austria and the Low Countries. Early examples of wheellocks are almost invariably ornate with the stock decorated with inlay of mother-of-pearl, steel, ivory, horn and occasionally precious metals. The steel of the locks themselves is engraved and chiselled into elaborate shapes, and many of them are outstanding works of art in their own right. The earlier pistols usually had a large ball at the end of the butt, probably to afford an easy grip for a horseman when drawing the pistol from the holster which was normally positioned at the front of the saddle.

Although the wheellock was made obsolete during the 17th century, it was not completely abandoned, and it is known that wheellocks were produced in parts of Europe until the late 17th and, in one or two areas, even as late as the early part of the 18th century. Wheellock hunting rifles were popular with the nobility for they afforded an excellent opportunity to display one's wealth and position by the amount of decoration.

During the long life of the wheellock certain changes are evident in the design. The earlier examples had very large lockplates. No doubt working on the principle that it was better to be safe than sorry, the early gunsmiths built safety devices into the mechanism, and later wheellocks may be recognised by the uncluttered

7 Sturdy German wheellock pistol of the latter part of the 16th century. The stock is nearly straight, and the large ball pommel was probably to ensure an easy grip for the user and not intended to be used as a club. The lockplate is large and has the usual safety catches. Barrel 13 inches. Bore .65 inch. K. Drake collection.

appearance of the lockplate after these safety catches were abandoned as superfluous. On the later locks the wheel is fitted on the inside of the lockplate, so that externally the only attachment is the doghead which is frequently chiselled and elaborately decorated. At first the rather excessive cost of the wheellock restricted its adoption; its use was limited to bodyguards and certain cavalry units, and it was never a 'general issue' weapon. During the wars of the 17th century some cavalry units obtained much less ornate weapons from northern Europe, particularly Holland. These had stocks which were normally completely plain and very simple steel locks.

Although the wheellock represented a vast improvement on the old matchlock, it also was not without fault. First of all it was mechanically complex: making the springs, wheels, small metal chains and sears required a degree of skill which was beyond that of the less competent metalworkers. The sheer complexity of the internal mechanism increased the possibility of mechanical failure, whilst dirt and breakages could more easily cause misfires or breakdowns. However, once the principle of mechanical ignition had been established, gunmakers from the early 16th century onwards were searching for simpler, easier, cheaper and possibly more efficient methods. In parts of Norway, Sweden and Denmark a type of lock was made, known, from its area of use, as the Baltic lock. It was in principle very similar to the wheellock in that sparks were produced by friction, but the method was far simpler. In the first place flint was used rather than pyrites, and this meant that it was just that little bit easier to obtain since flint has a wider natural occurrence. Secondly, in place of a complicated rotating wheel sparks were produced by friction between a simple steel plate and the sharpened edge of the piece of flint. This meant that internally the mechanism was much simpler, for the flint was held between the adjustable jaws of an arm, known as the cock, and the base of this pressed against a V-shaped spring. This removed the need for a complicated winding mechanism or a link, since the spring bore directly on the toe of the cock. The steel plate was situated at the end of a slightly curved arm which was secured at the other end to the lockplate and was tensioned by a spring. The vertical plate was placed above the pan and when the trigger was squeezed the pressure of the mainspring forced the cock to swing forward and scrape the flint down the face of the steel, producing the sparks of incandescent steel which fell into the pan to fire the priming and so ignite the main charge. This mechanism using flint and plate is known as the snaphaunce, the name being derived from the Dutch words 'snap hann' meaning 'snapping hen', and this was derived from the movement of the arm containing the flint. The basic action was made more sophisti-

cated by the fitting of an internal lever to operate the pan cover which had previously been pushed clear manually prior to firing.

The typical 17th-century Dutch snaphaunce lock was characterised by a large disc fitted at the end of a semicircular priming pan. In order to prevent the cock swinging too far forward, a block of metal, known as the buffer, was so positioned as to limit the swing of the cock and prevent it banging against the pan. To prepare the lock for firing, all that was required was to position the plate above the pan and then pull back the cock. This movement rotated a tumbler which pressed against the mainspring and so placed it under tension; at the same time a sear, fitted on the inside of the lockplate, projected through a drilled hole to engage with the rear end of the cock. This snapped into position and held the cock back under tension. Pressure on the trigger withdrew the sear and so allowed the spring to motivate the cock. The mechanics of the snaphaunce were far less complex than that of the wheellock, and as it was thus capable of easier massproduction quite considerable numbers of these locks were made. But it was soon outmoded by an improved version, and was therefore rendered obsolete at an early date.

Although abandoned by most gunmakers it continued to be used in two parts of the world for reasons which are not at all clear. In North Africa the Dutch form of the snaphaunce was in use right up until the early part of this century. Indeed the locks on many Moorish muskets are almost identical in design with the 17th-century Dutch version, and broadly speaking the only difference is one of quality. The manufacture of the snaphaunce also continued in northern Italy for,

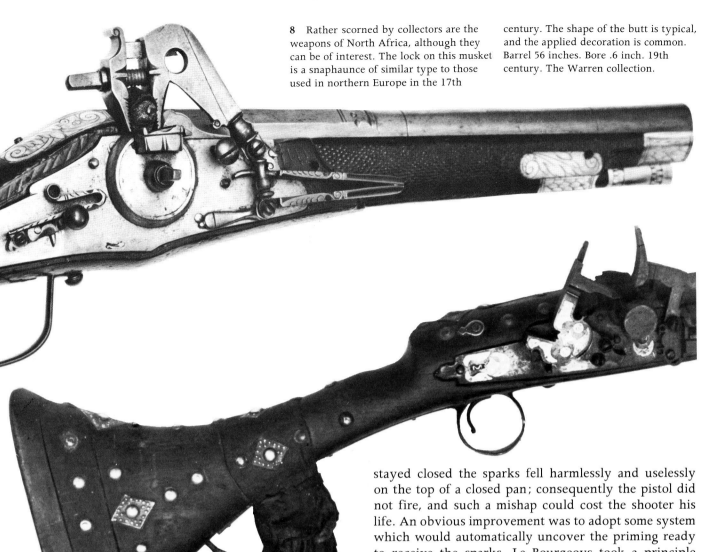

although it was obsolete by the middle of the 17th century, the metalworkers of Brescia produced pistols fitted with this form of lock until well into the early part of the 18th century. These Italian craftsmen were noted for the quality of their steelwork, and many of these snaphaunce pistols are indeed a delight because of the workmanship, which includes superb chiselling on the lock and plate as well as on the steel furniture.

It was a French gunsmith, Marin Le Bourgeoys, who improved on the basic snaphaunce principle to produce what was to become the standard method of ignition for the next two and a half centuries. If there was a serious drawback to the snaphaunce mechanism it was the necessity to push clear the pancover at the moment of firing. Normally this was done simply by connecting a lever from cock to pan, but there was always the danger that this might not function. If the pan cover stayed closed the sparks fell harmlessly and uselessly on the top of a closed pan; consequently the pistol did not fire, and such a mishap could cost the shooter his life. An obvious improvement was to adopt some system which would automatically uncover the priming ready to receive the sparks. Le Bourgeoys took a principle which is known to have been in use at a much earlier date, and produced an L-shaped piece of steel, usually known as the frizzen. Fitted above the pan the lower and smaller arm of the L-shaped piece served as the cover whilst the longer arm served as the steel. The frizzen was held in place by the tension of a small frizzen spring. As the cock swung forward the flint scraped down the long arm of the L so producing the sparks. At the same time the impact was sufficient to make the frizzen pivot upon the screw situated at the end of the short arm so uncovering the priming powder to receive the spark.

This in itself was not a new departure, and neither was the other feature which Marin Le Bourgeoys adopted. The normal arrangement with the sear acting upon the cock was for the arm to pass through a hole in the lockplate and engage with the base. This presented certain problems and was an inherent weakness of the mechanism. Le Bourgeoys took another system in which the cock was fitted to a shaped block of metal known as the tumbler, which was placed on the inside of the lockplate. Although the earliest examples differed, the usual system of affixing the cock was by means of a squared shank which projected through the lockplate and received the cock. The shaped section of the tumbler was so designed as to be engaged by the rear end of the mainspring. Pressing against the rear face of the tumbler

was a flat knife-like edge of the sear, under the pressure
of a small spring. As the tumbler was rotated the tip of
the sear engaged with a slot which was so designed and
so positioned that the sear, once engaged, could not be
removed by pressure on the trigger. This position,
known as the half cock, ensured that the weapon could
be carried in safety with little danger of an accidental
discharge. To prepare the pistol for firing the cock was
now pulled back a little further and this action disengaged the sear from the tumbler and allowed it to
engage with a second, shallower and slightly differently
angled slot further along the edge of the tumbler. In
this position, full cock, movement of the trigger would
withdraw the sear and so allow the pressure on the
mainspring, bearing directly on the tumbler, to drive
the cock forward, scraping the flint down the long face
of the frizzen to produce the sparks.

The French lock of Marin Le Bourgeoys combined
both these features, and it was to remain the model which
would continue in use until the middle of the 19th
century, indeed in some parts of the world right up
until the present century. The earliest flintlock as produced by Le Bourgeoys appears to have been made
about 1610, and there are a few specimens which can
be dated, with a fair degree of certainty, to this period.
The advantages of this system, with automatic pan cover
opening and use of the tumbler and sears with its full and
half cock position, were not at once widely adopted.

At first the use of the French lock does not appear to
have spread much beyond Paris where Le Bourgeoys
was working at that time.

By the mid 17th century the French lock was well
established and with one exception was to remain the
standard form of ignition for many years. The second
most popular form of ignition, which is not accepted
by some experts as a true flintlock, is the miguelet lock.
This form was developed primarily in the Mediterranean
area and was popular in Spain, parts of Italy and Sar-
dinia. It is found most commonly on Spanish pistols
and is easily distinguished by a number of features.
The cock is normally rather squat and angular in comparison with the graceful S-shape of the French style.
The jaws are rectangular and secured by a set-screw
which has, fitted at the top, a ring or pivoted bar which
enables the user to obtain a firm grip. This is necessary
because the mainspring on this type of lock is normally
quite powerful, and a good deal of strength is required
to cock it. The frizzen also tends to have a rather
rectangular shape, and most, but not all, have a vertically
grooved face. The other essentially and immediately
apparent difference is that, unlike the French version,
the mainspring is fitted on the outside of the lockplate.
The trigger and sear mechanism is very similar to that
on the snaphaunce, and the half and full cock positions
are engaged by means of sears which project through
holes in the lockplate. Miguelet locks are found on both

pistols and long arms, and the style remained in use until well into the 19th century. There are variations on this basic miguelet lock.

The French lock was used throughout the whole of Europe and America and can be found in many sizes and shapes. However, despite its very long working life, it is possible to date specimens within reasonable limits from changes in detail. In England a form of flintlock, known as the doglock, was produced during the 17th century. This is essentially the same as the French lock except that a safety position is secured by means of a small hook, the dog, which engages with a shaped recess cut on the back edge of the cock. Most specimens of this lock also have the buffer, as found on the snaphaunce.

As the gunmakers increased their technical ability the lock was modified to improve its action. In the very earliest examples the cock is secured to the tumbler by means of a nut and bolt passing through from the inside of the lock, but this was an unnecessarily complicated system. From a date quite early in the 17th century the cock was secured to the tumbler using much the same system as that on a wheellock. The tumbler was made

with a square-ended shank protruding through the lockplate; on to this slotted the cock with a corresponding square-cut hole, and a single screw held it firmly in position. On the earlier weapons the frizzen is mounted only by a single screw; but this did not make for easy movement, and soon a second arm to support the end of the frizzen screw was fitted on the lock. On the inside of the lockplate a bridle, or supporting arm, for the tumbler again improved the action. During the 17th century the lockplate and cock were generally flat-sided, but from the end of the 17th century onwards the lock assumed a concave shape, although the inside surface remained flat. Again as a generalisation it can be said that the size of the lock decreased; 17th-century examples tend to have fairly large lockplates, but the size was reduced over a period of a century until, by the end of the 18th, most of the lockplates are fairly small.

Towards the end of the 18th century there were further modifications intended to improve the efficiency of the lock. Small rollers were fitted where there was friction, most usually at the point where the arm of the frizzen pressed down on the frizzen spring. Sometimes a small roller was fitted at the end of the spring, sometimes at the end of the frizzen. Internally the mainspring was slightly modified so that instead of pressing directly on to the face of the tumbler, a small T-shaped bar was used to couple the end of the mainspring to the tumbler.

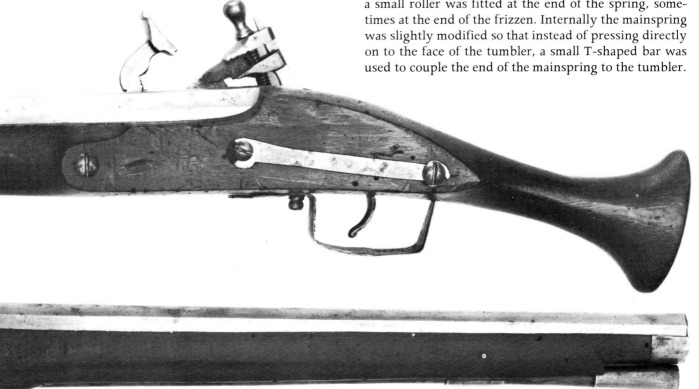

11 Not all wheellocks were covered with inlay, and the military versions were less elaborate although most still had some decoration. This example has some inlay and a gilded wheel cover. Barrel 13 inches. Bore .65 inch. Ken Drake collection.

12 Pair of French holster pistols with some gilding on the furniture. Decoration on continental pistols was, in general, more elaborate than that on English and American weapons. Barrel 10 inches. Bore .65 inch. The Warren collection.

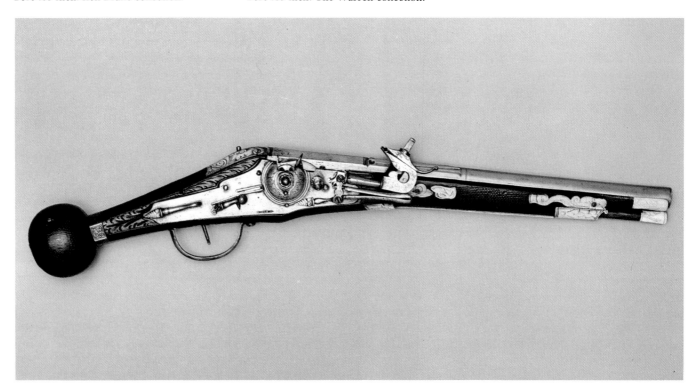

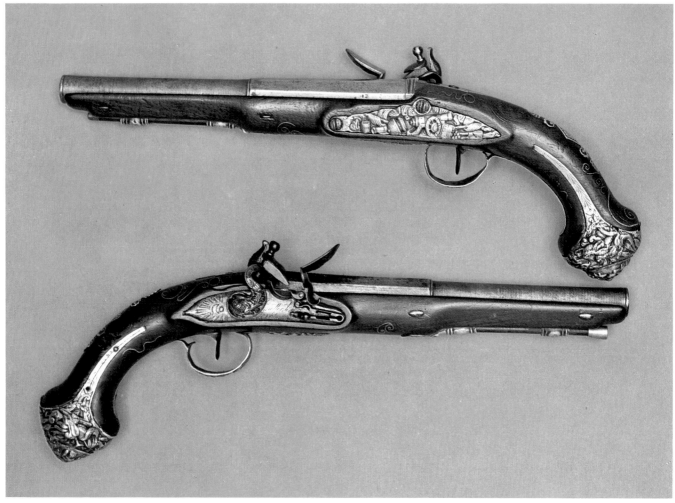

13 Pocket pistol by Grice of London. It is unusual in two respects: firstly because of the length of barrel, and secondly because the inlay is of steel and not silver. Barrel 8 inches. Bore .5 inch. The Warren collection.

14 Shooting birds on the wing was first introduced in the 18th century and soon became a passion with the leisured class. This typical print of 1804 shows, in the centre, a hunter loading his flintlock, whilst the figure on the left has just fired. The puff of smoke from the priming is clearly shown.

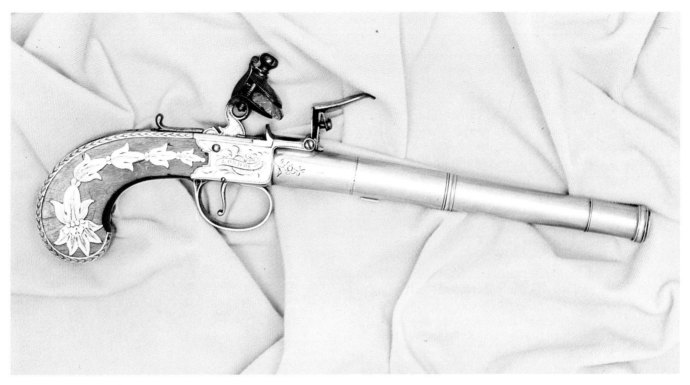

Since the area of metal in contact was smaller, friction was also reduced, and this helped to ensure a swifter, more positive action. Although the flintlock had the built-in safety position, the half cock, other extra safety devices were fitted. Possibly the most common, introduced in the 18th century, comprised a small sliding bar fitted into the lockplate and positioned just behind the cock. The inside face of the cock was cut with a corresponding slot so that, at the half cock position, the bar could be pushed forward to engage with the slot and so hold the lock safely in position.

Although the flintlock action was simple, efficient and generally satisfactory, it had, like previous systems, its limitations. Best quality flint was preferably black, but most contemporary authorities believed that it was only safe to rely on thirty strikes from a flint before it was worn out. It was quite possible to get more and, on poor quality flint, far less, but thirty was reckoned to be a safe average. Then too there was the wear on the frizzen, for on a hunting weapon in constant use the face became worn, and on well used weapons it may be found that the frizzen has been either replaced or refaced. Like the wheellock and snaphaunce before it, the flintlock was somewhat at the mercy of the weather, for priming could become damp or dispersed by a breeze, but for the hunter even more serious was the hangfire. Quite apart from the time taken for the bullet to pass from the muzzle of the gun to the target, there was a further, and appreciable, delay between the pressing of the trigger and the actual explosion of the powder. It took a small, but nevertheless measurable, time for the flint to swing forward and strike sparks, for the sparks to fall into the pan, the priming to take fire, the flame to pass from the pan through the touch hole to the main charge of powder and for that to burn and expel the bullet. Thus the hunter had to make two allowances, one for the hangfire and one for the speed of the moving target. Efforts to overcome this problem were numerous, and there were minor improvements in the design of the chamber and the breech to ensure rapid combustion of the powder. The use of gold or platinum to prevent the touch hole fouling up with the waste products of the explosion had some minimal effect, but it was apparent to many that the flintlock had more or less reached the limit of its capabilities.

In Scotland, in the small village of Belhelvie, a little to the north of Aberdeen, lived an obscure but intelligent Scottish clergyman, Alexander Forsyth. Apart from his pastoral duties he had many outside interests. He was a keen shooter, and he too pondered on the problem of the hangfire. He was also interested in science, and at some time during his chemical studies he had become familiar with the qualities of fulminates. These unstable chemical compounds require only a sharp blow to produce an explosion. Experiments had been made using

fulminates in place of gunpowder, but they had not proved very successful. Forsyth took the idea a step further and, instead of using them simply as a substitute for gunpowder, he tried using them as a means of ignition. The exploding fulminate produced an appreciable spark, and he felt that this could well be used to ignite the main charge. His problems were how to apply the fulminate, only a small quantity of which was needed, to the right place, and how to discharge it with absolute safety. His answer was ingenious, if somewhat complex, and from its shape the device is usually known as the Forsyth scent bottle. Basically it was a small metal container which held a tiny quantity of fulminate. From one end projected a small spout, from the other a metal spring-loaded plunger. To operate the mechanism the scent bottle was inverted, allowing a few grains of powder to fall out in position near the touch hole. When the scent bottle was reversed this brought the spring-operated plunger into position, one end situated just above the grains of fulminate. In place of the flintlock cock a solid-nosed hammer was substituted, and when this came down it banged down the spring plunger which struck the fulminate crystals and thus produced the explosion, the flash of which detonated the gunpowder.

In 1807 he patented the idea but, although his system was quite practical and was fitted to a number of guns, it was not an ideal solution. The scent bottle was quite complex, and its design involved a certain danger in that a quantity of fulminate was stored very close to the point of detonation. However, the principle had now

15 A double barrelled flintlock pistol which has been converted to the percussion system and has suffered in the process. It is nevertheless still of interest and could be greatly improved with some skilled restoration. Barrel 9½ inches. About 1830. The Warren collection.

been clearly demonstrated. Forsyth tried hard to interest the Ordnance, who supplied firearms to the British army, in his invention, and for a while he carried out some research and work in the Tower of London; but his results were received with very little enthusiasm.

Other gunsmiths saw the potential of the system and appreciated its weaknesses, and they sought some means to apply the fulminate to the touch hole in an easily packaged, easily handled form. Small quantities of fulminates were enclosed in all manner of receptacles and containers. Some used quills; one end of the small tube holding the fulminate was placed inside the touch hole whilst the other end was banged down with the hammer. Others produced systems whereby the fulminate was compounded into tiny balls and these were placed over the touch hole. There were rolls, reminiscent of children's rolls of caps, with the small blobs of fulminate positioned in thin paper sheets, and there were even thin metal foil caps. Again most of these systems worked, and weapons using them were produced; but they were limited. Fitting the caps into place called for a degree of dexterity which was not always practical, especially under conditions of active service or hunting in the field. Experiments were continued to find an improved system, and the one which proved to be the most practical was the copper percussion cap.

There is much dispute as to who was the original designer of this system, and there were a number of claimants to the honour; but whoever it was, the system was in general use by the 1820s. The copper closed-

ended tube was a quarter of an inch or so long, with corrugated sides which allowed a fairly tight fit, and at the closed end was deposited a small quantity of fulminate. The firearm designed to use these caps had a small metal tube fitted into the breech. The small tube was drilled through and so situated that it was struck by the solid-nosed hammer. Over this tube, the nipple, was placed the copper cap. When the hammer fell it struck the cap which was forced home against the end of the nipple to produce an explosion and a flash which passed through the nipple into the breech and so fired the charge. In the interests of safety the nose of the hammer was usually recessed so that as it came down the nipple was totally enclosed by the hammer head before the solid section struck the cap. This simple arrangement ensured that if the cap splintered it did not fly off in all directions.

The percussion cap had many advantages. First of all it was of a reasonable size and could be placed on the nipple quite easily. It was safe and reliable, and even in the event of a misfire the cap could be quickly removed and a fresh one substituted.

With the appearance of the percussion cap the circumstances were now ripe for the rapid development of modern firearms. The cap simplified ignition, for it dispensed with the bulky frizzen and the necessity for changing flints and substituted for it a simple mechanism with a quick, very reliable action. It facilitated the construction of all manner of weapons, and from the 1830s onwards the revolver came into its own.

16 *top* German wheellock pistol of the late 16th century. The stock is inlaid with intricate floral patterns and birds. Barrel 13 inches. Bore .64 inch. *bottom* Early 17th-century wheellock with inlaid walnut stock, engraved lockplate and chiselled cock. Barrel 34 inches. Bore .66 inch. T. H. Porter collection.

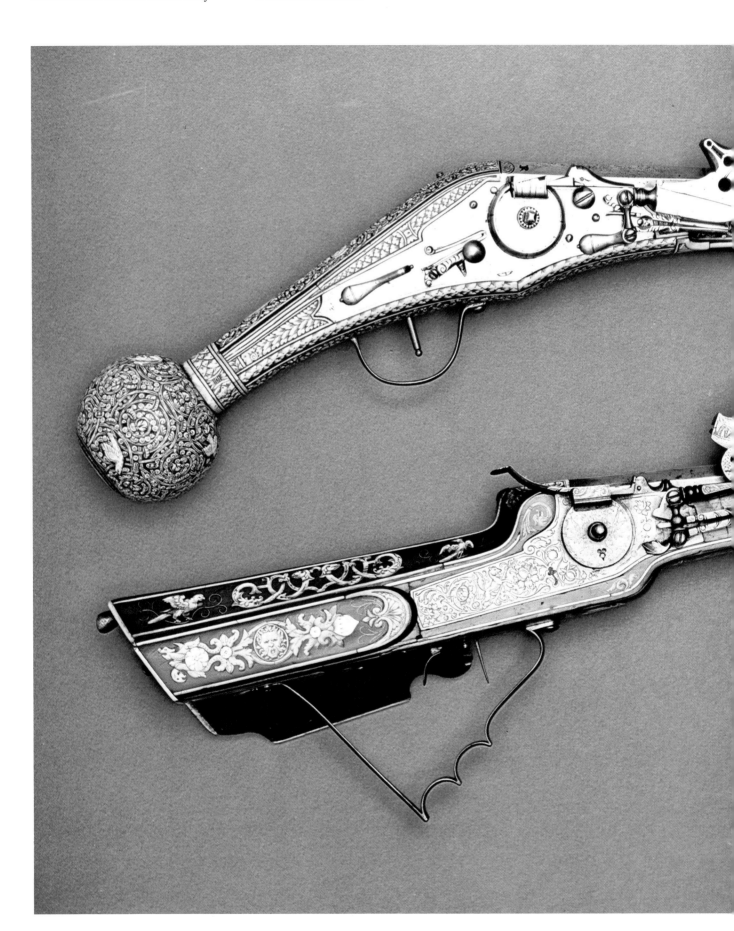

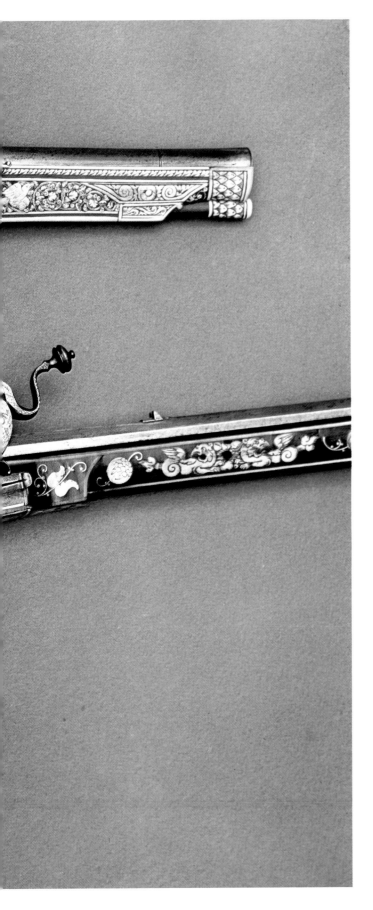

Revolvers were by no means a new idea, for there had been wheellock, snaphaunce and flintlock revolvers, but all had been handicapped by the necessity for fitting frizzens or cocks to the various chambers in the cylinder. The percussion cap made life much easier since these appendages were no longer necessary. What was more important was that the concept of chemical ignition had been introduced, and gunmakers all over Europe began experimenting with various systems which utilised the fulminate. A logical step was to integrate primer and explosive into one unit, the cartridge. Cartridges were not new, for they had been used from the 16th century onwards, but very few attempts had ever been made to incorporate their own means of ignition. Now there were many experiments, but the first really practical system came in 1835 when a Frenchman, Lefaucheux, introduced his pinfire cartridge. Essentially it consisted of a paper case with a brass head, and inside the head was situated a small percussion cap. From the cap there extended a plunger or pin, and when the cartridge was placed inside the breech the pin projected through a little slot in the breech. When the hammer fell it hit the pin which in turn struck the cap, and since this was situated inside the powder there was rapid ignition. Here was a clear pointer to the future development, and by 1860 after various experiments the American firm of Smith & Wesson produced the first of the rimfire cartridges. These had metal cases with a raised rim around the end, and inside this rim was deposited a small amount of fulminate. The specially shaped hammer of the gun struck against the rim of the cartridge and so produced the flash to ignite the charge. By the 1860s the rimfire cartridge was being produced in quantity, and many weapons were made to take it.

At the same time another system was being explored, which was to be the one that became generally adopted – the centrefire cartridge. Soon complete metal cases were being made, and by the 1870s the modern cartridge as we know it, with a metal case, central primer and a shaped bullet, was in general use. Since the appearance of the centrefire cartridge developments in firearms have mostly been in the fields of improved propellants and the size and shape of the bullet.

Concurrent with the development of the metal cartridge was the introduction of breech-loading firearms. Most flintlock and wheellock weapons were muzzle loading, where powder and ball had to be inserted by way of the muzzle. Numerous attempts had been made to adopt a simpler and more convenient method of loading in powder and ball at the breech, but, with few exceptions, all had proved deficient in some way or other. It was only with the appearance of the Smith & Wesson revolver, using a .22 inch bullet that breech-loading revolvers became a really practical proposition.

23

What to collect

The choice open to the collector of antique firearms is, at one and the same time, enormous and yet limited. Obviously the choice of any particular field must depend upon the available resources. For someone with large financial reserves there is scope for the collecting of wheellocks, breech-loading flintlock pistols and all manner of choice specimens, but for the collector of more restricted resources such items are automatically excluded. For the real beginner the choice is certainly restricted, and today very few pistols of any quality are available at less than £30 (US $75), while £100 (US $250) is more likely to be the average sort of working figure.

However, forgetting the unforgettable, that is ignoring the restrictions placed upon one by the cash available, what are the possibilities? There are, of course, a large number of collectors who are totally indiscriminate in the sense of not restricting themselves to any one particular type of weapon. There are those who will cheerfully purchase a percussion rifle, a flintlock pocket pistol and a North African musket, and gain equal pleasure from all three. There are others who will want to concentrate on one particular field, but this is very much a matter of personal preference; there is no right or wrong approach. In exactly the same way there are collectors who insist that collecting is only worth while if one obtains the best possible specimen of any particular type, whilst others say that it is more enjoyable to have a number of possibly indifferent examples of a wide range of weapons. Again this is very much a personal choice.

Ignoring, then, the question of cash, what can one collect? Although the dividing lines are often indistinct, the majority of firearms can be broken down into fairly broad classifications, and it might be worth while considering each of these groups.

Matchlocks

The type of matchlocks, the earliest form of firearm, that most collectors are ever likely to own will come from the East, for European matchlocks are extremely rare and invariably very expensive. When European explorers of the 16th century, Portuguese, Spanish and British, ventured on to the then unknown oceans, they took with them matchlock muskets and wheellock

pistols, and the first acquaintance of any natives, such as the Japanese and the Indians, with firearms was with these weapons. The virtues of the matchlock, its simplicity and cheapness of construction ensured that it remained popular with the less industrialised countries. In India the matchlock was to continue in use right up to the early part of this century, and generally speaking the Indian matchlock is known as a torador or bundook. On these weapons the serpentine operates differently from that of the Western version with the arm swinging forward towards the touch hole, away from the shooter, exactly the opposite to the system most commonly used on the European muskets. In addition the barrels tend to be very much longer and smaller bored than their European counterparts. The stocks on most of the Indian ones are very straight with only a slight droop to the butt, which is usually fairly basic in shape and lacks the deep curving heel common on most European ones. Often the barrel on the Indian matchlock is beautifully carved and chiselled and is secured to the stock either by metal bands, capuchins, or by thongs of rawhide. Triggers and muzzles are often finely chiselled, frequently in the form of animals. A few matchlocks with very pronounced curved butts are found; this shape originated in the northern part of India and is usually known as an Afghan stock, but in fact they come from Sind.

Japan too retained the matchlock long after it had been abandoned in Europe, and again it acquired certain national characteristics. Japanese matchlocks are generally fitted with short, very heavy barrels with a beautifully polished, sturdy wooden stock and will sometimes be found with a snaplock fitted. This means that the serpentine holding the match is at rest with the arm pressing down into the pan. To set the action the cock is raised and is held in this position by a sear which is withdrawn by the action of the trigger. This type of mechanism was also fitted to some early European muskets but was not popular because of the possibility of accidental discharge. The triggers are usually in the form of a button and, like the Indian ones, lack a trigger guard. Barrels are often inlaid with simple but pleasing designs and patterns. The Japanese, despite their incredible command of metallurgy, seem always to have had difficulty with the manufacture of springs, and most Japanese matchlocks are fitted with brass springs which

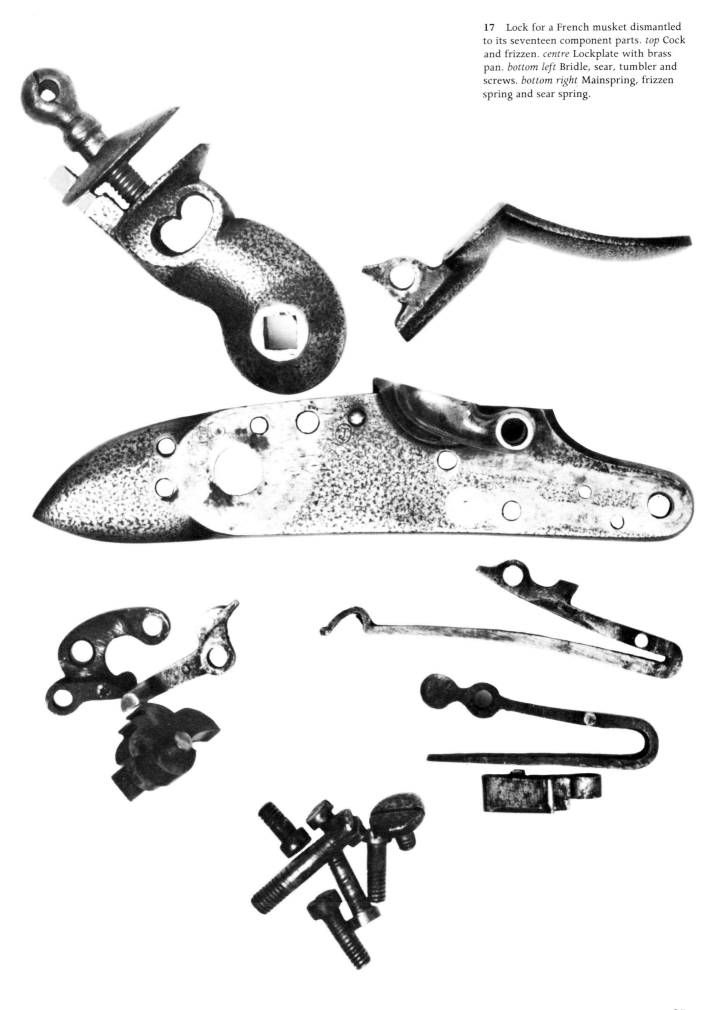

18   Light sporting wheellock gun known
as a tschinke. These were manufactured in
the area of the Czechoslovak-Polish border.
The mainspring is mounted externally.
Jagdmuseum, Munich.

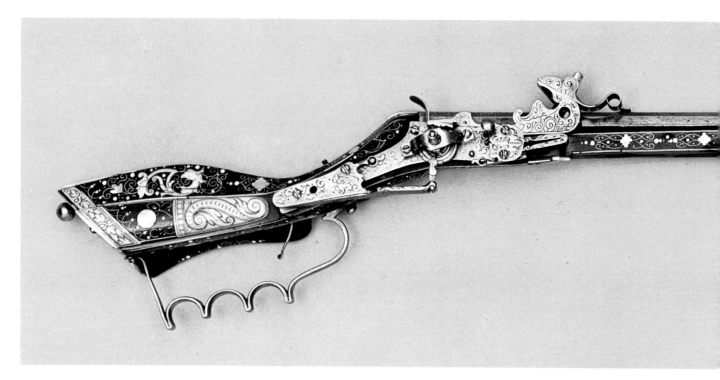

tend to give the action a rather soggy feel. One novelty in this field are the very small Japanese matchlocks, only some four or five inches long. These are not toys in the strict sense of the word but were made for the Festival of Boys, when it was traditional to make presents to the boy of the household, and such gifts often included miniature arms and armour.

Until fairly recently Indian matchlocks have been rather scorned by collectors, but there are signs of an increasing demand. Japanese weapons are enjoying a high demand; good quality pieces are being much sought after and prices have risen substantially over the last few years.

Wheellocks

As a group the wheellocks are, as regards decoration, the most aesthetically pleasing of all firearms. The early pistols with their inlay of mother-of-pearl, ivory and steel are extremely attractive, and they are also quite rare, two factors that combine to ensure that they are also invariably very expensive. The early pistols, with large ball butts, are beyond the pocket of the average collector, but there is always the possibility that one will discover a 'sleeper', an undiscovered treasure, in an antique shop or on a junk stall, so hope should never be abandoned. The later 17th-century wheellocks, the more military type, are very plain with a simple stock, steel trigger guard, steel butt cap and very plain lock. These are certainly more common and slightly less expensive, but it is very much a matter of degree. Long wheellock hunting rifles which were produced until well into the 17th century, and possibly in some parts

of Europe even into the 18th century, are extremely attractive with their polished walnut stocks and inlay, but again they are expensive. The shape of the butt is unusual, for it was designed to be held not against the shoulder as in most long arms but against the side of the face when aiming and firing. The recoil was effectively reduced by the very thick, almost invariably octagonal barrels. On most of these weapons there are apparently two triggers; the rear one is the normal one, and the one in front is the hair trigger. These have a series of small springs and levers so adjusted that once set only the merest pressure is required to operate the mechanism. The virtue of a hair trigger was that heavy pressure on the trigger could throw the weapon off aim.

Identification of wheellocks is largely academic: the great majority of them are of German origin although some were manufactured in Hungary, Italy and France. The French ones are distinguished by their method of construction, with the mainspring fitted into the stock rather than on the plate as with the majority of others. Then too there is the very characteristic and undoubtedly attractive light fowling piece known as the 'tschinke'. These wheellocks are characterised by a number of features: lightness, the sharp, almost hockey-stick shape of the butt, the moulded trigger guard and general decoration. The tschinke was manufactured mostly in the Czech/Polish border region and gets its name from the town of Teschen in the area where they were very popular; they are sometimes known as Silesian pieces. During the 17th century some much plainer long arms were produced, but these frequently have carved and chiselled locks even if the butts are quite plain. These

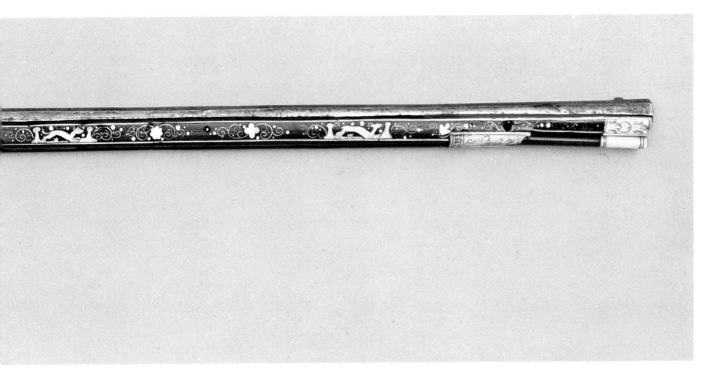

later weapons are also characterised by the plain uncluttered lockplate, for the wheel was mounted internally.

Snaphaunces

As a group snaphaunces are one of the scarcest of antique firearms, for the system only had a short working life, and very few early examples have survived. Weapons with a Baltic lock are extremely rare. The Dutch form of lock, with its large and angular appearance, survived up until a few years ago on North African muskets. However, it is unlikely that anyone would confuse the genuine 17th-century piece with the much later Moorish locks, for their general standard of workmanship bears little or no comparison with the earlier examples. The vast majority of snaphaunce pistols which turn up in the market are of Italian origin, produced in the northern part of the country around Brescia, until well into the 18th century. They have a fairly characteristic appearance with a rather slender, slightly sloping butt and a pommel reminiscent of an onion in shape. The lock and barrels are frequently chiselled and carved, and the stocks inlaid with superb quality cut steel. If the locks are removed a date will often be found inscribed on the inside of the lockplate. Rarer still are those Scottish pistols which were fitted with snaphaunce locks until the last quarter of the 17th century; needless to say every specimen will be expensive.

The flintlock

For all except the very wealthy or extremely lucky collector the flintlock is likely to be the earliest type of action that one can hope to acquire. Fortunately the flintlock mechanism had a working life of 250 years; it was produced in every size and in a variety of designs and was fitted to many weapons throughout this period. Flintlock firearms developed certain national characteristics, so that the field for the flintlock collector is extremely broad. Indeed it is so wide that it is totally impossible to cover it adequately within the limits of a brief chapter such as this. Probably the only practical approach is to break the field into sections and deal briefly with each.

Flintlock pistols

The earliest available flintlock pistols date from the first half of the 17th century, but such weapons are comparatively rare although a few specimens do appear in auction rooms or in the hands of some dealers. The great majority of these early flintlock pistols were fitted with a long barrel, the bore of which is fairly small. They are also characterised by a number of moulded ridges or rings around the muzzle. Many early pistols also have the barrel stepped, a feature which continued into the 18th century; at the breech, where maximum strength is required, it is usually octagonal and thick-walled, but this shaping changes part of the way along and becomes four-sided, eventually converting to circular section at the muzzle end. Early flintlock pistols have stocks which are usually plain and butts which are oval in section and have a square-cut end, often bound with a steel band, but it is not unusual to find ball-shaped pommels on some of these early examples. The lock itself is characterised, usually, by a fairly

19, 20 Double barrelled pistol by W. Parker of London. It has a platinum lined touch hole and refinements such as the rollers fitted to the tip of the frizzen springs. This shape of cock is often found on Parker's pistols. Barrel 10 inches. Bore .65 inch. About 1810. A. J. Galloway collection.

slender cock, and both cock and lockplate are commonly rectangular in section. The dog catch, mentioned above, may be found fitted to pistols, blunderbusses and long arms.

During the latter part of the 17th century barrels were slightly reduced in length, the butts became more round in section, and there began to appear one of the characteristic features of the flintlock pistol, the swelling at the base of the butt, the pommel. At the end of the 17th century and in the early 18th, the pommel was frequently fitted with a metal cap, and this was continued up the side of the butt by two long narrow arms, known as spurs. The butt cap itself was frequently embellished with grotesque masks and was most commonly of brass or steel but occasionally silver; on rare occasions gilt was used. The slope of the butt really altered but little, and the stock itself often carried some simple carving, usually no more than moulding around the rear extension of the breech, the tang, which was slotted into the stock and secured by a screw. Trigger guards on these pistols tend to be fairly broad and are normally of the same metal as the butt cap. The ramrod, used to drive home the ball, was housed in the stock beneath the barrel and was usually held in place by one or more metal tubes, the ramrod pipes, again normally of the same metal as the butt cap and trigger guard. These pipes are actually let into the stock below the barrel.

The shape of the lock also gives a general indication of date, for at the turn of the 17th century it had acquired a somewhat drooping banana shape, tapering to a point at either end, whilst its cross-section is generally concave on the outside. The graceful cock of this period was normally concave in section, and the whole pistol of the early 18th century still retained some of the features of the 17th century with a moderately long barrel and substantial stock. During the 18th century the lock lost its banana-shape and became straighter and simpler. Military pistols of the 18th century are normally somewhat more conservative as far as changes of style are concerned. As the 18th century progressed the tendency was for the side spurs to be reduced in length, but whereas the civilian pistol had largely abandoned them at the end of the 18th century military pistols still retained a butt cap with very attenuated spurs. Another useful feature in general dating is the trigger: on pistols of the late 17th and early 18th centuries the triggers are normally fairly flat and broad and frequently have a backward curling tip.

The military pistols of the 18th century were of plain rugged construction. A circular barrel, externally tapering slightly from breech to muzzle, was secured to the stock by the tang screw which again is another dating feature. On the earlier flintlock weapons the screw engaging the tang is inserted from below the stock, that is it goes up from inside or just in front of the trigger

21 Butt and lock of an Indian matchlock. Weapons such as this were used until comparatively recently; the quality varies enormously, ranging from superb to basic. T. H. Porter collection.

22 When a new system of ignition was adopted there was often a period of overlap when two systems were used together. This weapon has a lock which is fitted on the left with a matchlock and on the right with a wheellock. T. H. Porter collection.

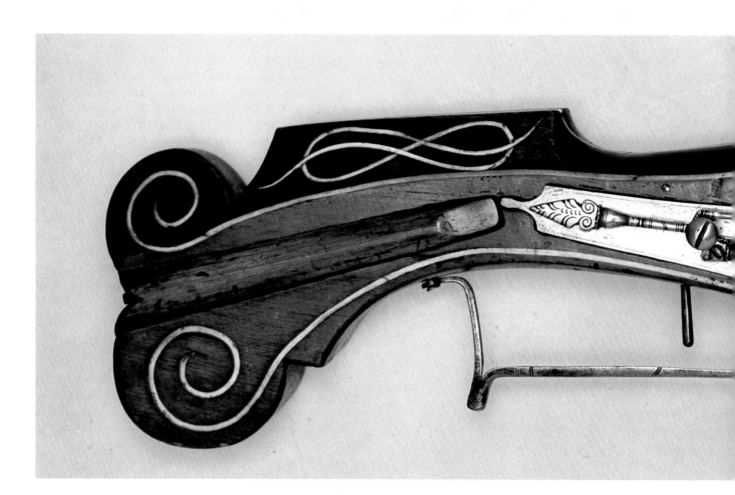

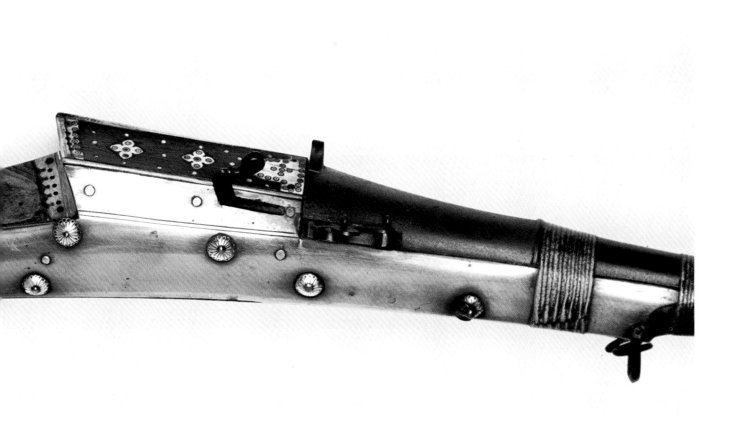

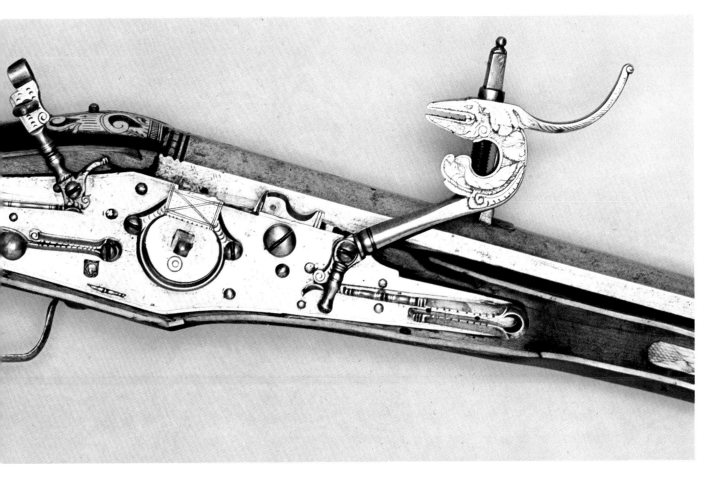

23 American martial pistol, model of 1836, produced by R. Johnson of Middletown, Connecticut. It has a swivel ramrod, a brass pan and a barrel secured to the black walnut stock by a band and screw. Barrel 8½ inches. Bore .54 inch. J. Jarvis collection.

24 Detail of 23. Military firearms were normally examined before being accepted by the government, and the inspector placed his mark somewhere on the weapon. The larger stamp has the initials WAT, probably those of Captain William Anderson Thornton whose mark appears on a whole range of U.S. martial arms.

guard, through the stock to engage with the tang. This feature disappeared early in the 18th century and was replaced by a screw inserted through the top of the tang, an obvious simplification of construction. Barrels were secured to the stock by a series of pins, usually two or three, which passed through the wooden stock to engage with the holes cut into lugs secured to the bottom of the barrel. The trigger guard and ramrod pipes were similarly secured, whereas the butt cap was often held in place by a large screw. The lock was secured to the stock by a screw which passed through the wood from the side opposite to the lock. In order to give a greater strength and a solid base on which the head of the screw might bite, a side plate was fitted. Normally on the military pistols this was quite plain and usually of brass, although on some civilian pistols the side plates were frequently very ornate. As a broad generalisation it can be said that the length of barrel of pistols was reduced during the 18th century.

Military weapons were normally distinguished by some markings, in the case of British weapons most commonly the royal cipher made up of a crown with the initials of the sovereign: J.R. for James II (reigned 1685–1688), W.R. for William III (1689–1702), A.R. for Anne (1702–1714), G.R. for any of the Georges I to IV (1714–1830), W.R. for William IV (1830–1837) and V.R. for Victoria (1837–1901). British military weapons also had the word 'Tower' engraved on the lockplate, indicating that they were accepted as official weapons, and up until 1764 the date was also engraved on the tail of the lockplate. This practice was abandoned because it was found that armourers and others were reluctant to accept locks which, by the date, seemed to suggest that they had been in store for some time. This decision is regretted by all later collectors! The earliest dates known to appear on these pistols are from the 1720s and the latest is 1764. Many of the official military flintlock pistols bear some form of regimental marking, usually engraved on the barrel, but the titles are abbreviated: thus 'R.H.G.' stands for the Royal Horse Guards. Sometimes numbers occur, and these may well represent a squadron, the platoon, ship or rack as well as the number of the actual weapon.

Ramrods are normally quite plain and of wood with a brass tip, although metal ones were later substituted. Towards the end of the 18th century the captive, or swivel, ramrod made its appearance, for in the heat of battle it was very easy to lose the ramrod, and without this the weapon was virtually useless. A small lug was fitted beneath the muzzle; through this went a screw which held in place a twin link with a crossbar, and the ramrod was fitted through this crossbar. The swivel was ingeniously shaped so that the ramrod could be driven home into the housing beneath the barrel or equally well withdrawn and used to ram down the ball loading the weapon.

Queen Anne pistols

Although the name might seem to suggest that these weapons date from the early 18th century this is far from being the case. This generic collector's term covers pistols which were manufactured from the reign of Queen Anne until well into the 1770s and 1780s. There are a number of variations within the group, but basically they may be described as having a graceful curved butt, usually fitted with a silver cap embossed into the form of a grotesque face, human or animal, or less often incorporating some other feature such as a coat of arms. The butt is often plain but might equally well be decorated with silver wire inlay, a characteristic form of decoration on pistols of this type. To do this the gunmaker chiselled very small channels into the wood, usually in the form of volutes and arabesques, and into these channels was placed soft silver wire. This was very gently tapped causing it to swell and grip the inside of the channel to form a very pleasing decoration. Also set into the butt near the top there is usually a small metal shield of silver or brass, which is known as the escutcheon and on which could be engraved the owner's initials or arms.

The most characteristic features of these pistols are probably the lock and barrel, for they have the lock

25 The lock of this wheellock demonstrates the skill of the smiths in the quality of the chiselling and engraving on the metalwork. There is a hair trigger to

facilitate steadiness of aiming. The weapon bears the name JOHANN JACOB BAHR IN WURTZBURG. Bayerische Nationalmuseum, Munich.

26 Inlaid butt of a German wheellock smooth bore carbine of the mid 16th century, with typical decorative themes. T. H. Porter collection.

mounted directly on to the breech with no separate plate, but lock, breech and barrel are made in one. Many of these pistols have only a butt of wood, although some are made with a half stock which extends part of the way along the barrel. The cock is normally graceful and rather S-shaped; the frizzen spring is mounted on the outside of the barrel with a characteristic up-swinging shape. A side plate is frequently fitted, but this may serve little practical purpose and is largely decorative.

Some of these Queen Anne pistols use the boxlock where the cock is mounted centrally at the breech. The majority of these pistols have a barrel, known from its shape as a 'cannon barrel', which is screwed off for loading, so that powder and bullet can be placed directly into the breech. Most of these Queen Anne pistols, therefore, do not have a ramrod; but on some the barrel does not unscrew, and these have a ramrod, usually of steel, fitted beneath the barrel. Queen Anne pistols vary enormously in size, ranging from full sized holster pistols to quite small pocket pistols.

Pocket pistols

One of the great virtues of the wheellock and flintlock mechanisms was that they could be manufactured to any size and could therefore be fitted to weapons small enough to fit conveniently into the pocket and thus suitable for personal defence. There then developed a group of small pistols which are usually lumped together under the designation of pocket pistols. Those of the 17th century are essentially scaled-down versions of the holster pistol but with the characteristic that they have a small ball trigger and no trigger guard. During the 18th century a common pocket pistol design was evolved which was small and had a special form of flintlock. In order to prevent the weapon snagging on clothing when being drawn in a hurry at a moment of crisis, the lock was mounted centrally above the breech; this arrangement was known as the boxlock. The cock and frizzen were set centrally with the touch hole drilled through the top of the barrel and the frizzen spring so designed as to fit more or less flush with the top of the barrel. Early pocket pistols have much the same shaped butt as the Queen Annes, slightly round or oval in section, but during the latter part of the 18th century the slab-sided butt was increasingly adopted. It was cheaper and easier to manufacture, for it consisted of a slab of wood, rectangular in section, cut to a convenient shape.

Since these pistols were to be carried in the pocket it was obviously essential that some safety mechanism be fitted, and on most there may be one or even two such devices. Many of the later 18th-century flintlock pocket pistols have a concealed trigger so that with the cock in the half cock position the straight trigger sets

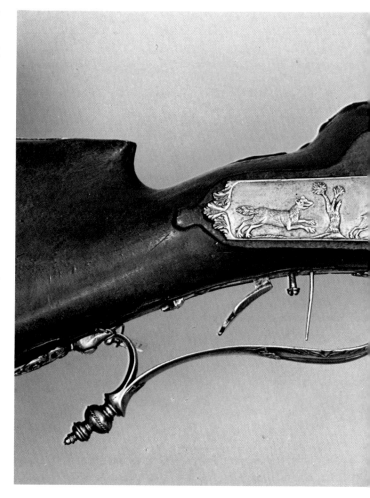

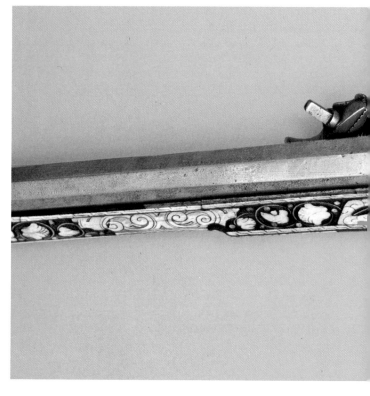

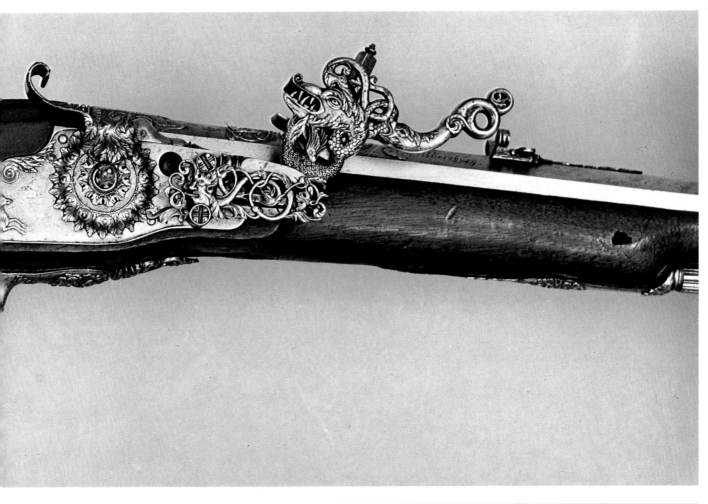

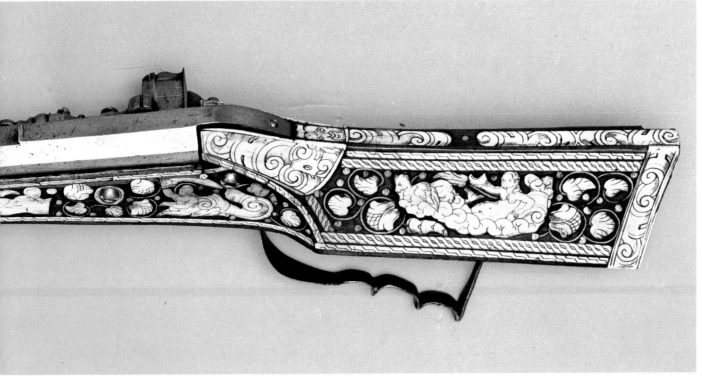

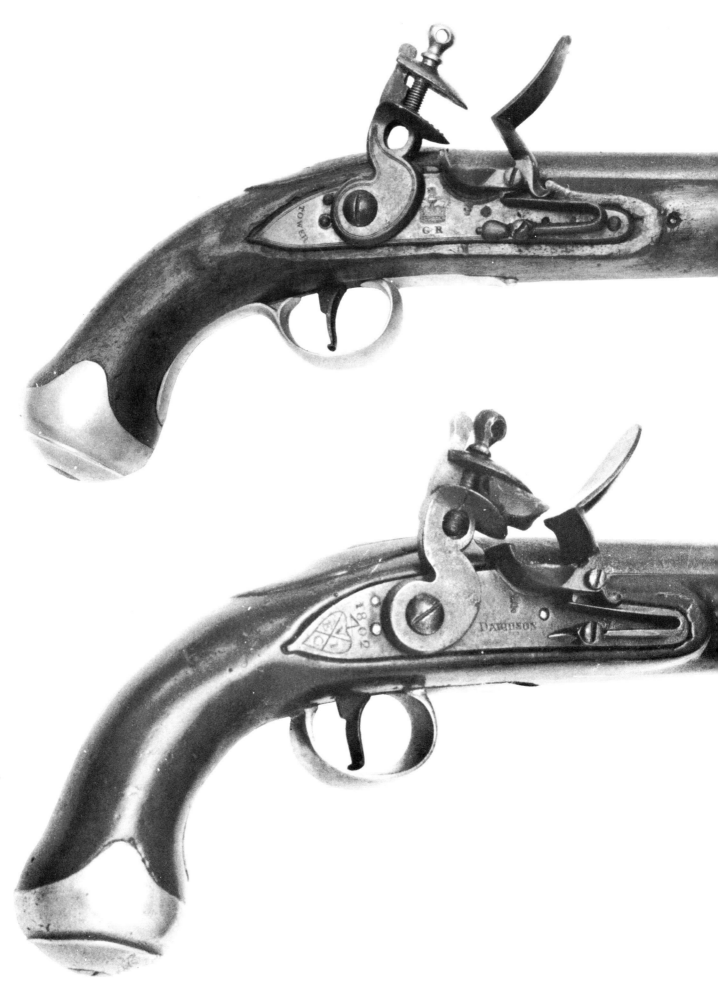

27   This British Army issue pistol is very similar to the one in plate 28. It bears on the lockplate the word TOWER and a crowned G.R. A comparison of the two pictures will reveal that the general quality of this pistol is slightly better than the East India Company one. Barrel 9 inches. Bore .65 inch. G. Kellam collection.

28   Military flintlock pistol made by Joseph Davidson and dated 1802. The lockplate bears the mark of the East India Company, a heart quartered, with the initials VEIC. It is simple but sturdy and is similar to those pistols used by the British Army. Barrel 9 inches. Bore .65 inch. G. Kellam collection.

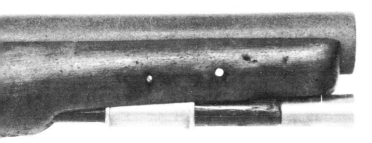

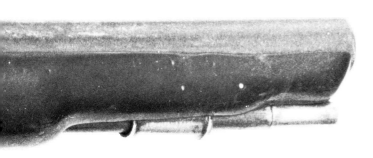

flush within the bottom of the breech. When the cock is brought back to the full cock position the trigger is automatically dropped down down into the position ready for firing. This removed the need for a trigger guard, an arrangement which also helped to give a smoother outline to the pistol. In addition there was a top safety catch fitted to lie flush with the top of the butt and breech. The bar was slotted around the cock and terminated in a small forward-projecting spike. With the pan closed and the cock in half cock position, the safety catch was pushed forward, and the spike passed through a hole in the rear of the pan and engaged with another hole in the base of the frizzen, so locking this down; at the same time the other end of the bar engaged with a notch at the rear of the cock, locking this into position. Less common is the sliding trigger guard found on late 18th-century pocket pistols which can be moved to lock the mechanism in the half cock position.

Since the great majority of pocket pistols have detachable barrels there is no need for a ramrod to be fitted. To remove the barrel some form of key was used, and on many barrels there is a small lug situated at the base of the breech; a circular key with a corresponding slot slipped over the barrel to engage with this lug, so offering a good purchase when removing or replacing the barrel. Another variety of key was a four-sided, slightly tapering bar which was pushed into the barrel to engage with notches cut into the inside of the muzzle. One very rare variation of design, found only on pistols of the late 17th century, has a screw-off barrel which is permanently linked to the breech by means of a small metal arm, so that the barrel could be unscrewed but was safe from accidental loss.

Duelling pistols

During the latter part of the 18th century the sword was largely replaced by the pistol as the weapon of that ritual test of honour, the duel. At first, presumably, any available pistols were used in these murderous encounters, but gunsmiths were no doubt approached and asked to produce pistols especially designed for the duel. Towards the latter part of the 18th century the duelling pistol was fully developed. There were numerous minor variations, but basically the common feature of these weapons was an octagonal barrel, made heavy to reduce recoil and fitted to a fairly plain stock. The butt usually carried some cross-hatching to afford a firm grip and had a rather hockeystick-shape to it. The trigger guard frequently had a spur fitted at the rear, so that the butt was gripped with the thumb and two fingers while the second finger was around the spur and the index finger was through the trigger guard, so ensuring a firm steady hold. These pistols are fitted with sights, but English pistols are very seldom rifled,

29 Detail of a ball butt typical of the highly decorative wheellock pistols produced in Nuremberg during the second half of the 16th century. T. H. Porter collection.

30 Plainer 17th-century wheellock with large engraved lockplate. The shaped trigger guard encloses a normal as well as a set trigger. Decoration is largely confined to simple carving. T. H. Porter collection.

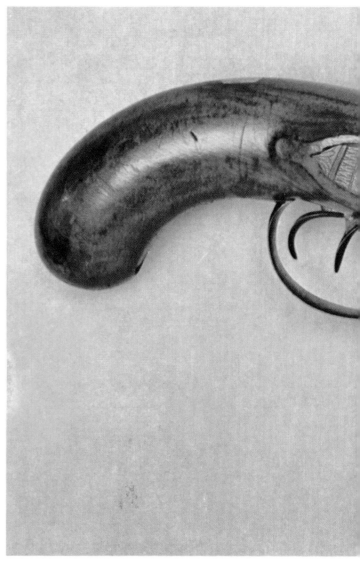

for it was not considered good form to use such a weapon. In order that each participant should have an equal chance duelling pistols were supplied in matched pairs, and the code of duelling allowed the choice to be made by the challenged party. Duelling pistols were sold in a wooden case, usually of oak or mahogany; the inside space was lined with baize and was divided by a number of partitions into compartments of various shapes to hold the pistols, bullet mould, screwdrivers, powder flask, cleaning rods, patches and a variety of optional extras to suit the purchaser's taste. The lids of many of these cases have a small inset metal escutcheon as well as a carrying handle.

The locks of the pistols usually incorporate all the most up-to-date mechanical features and refinements such as platinum- or gold-lined touch holes and pans. The use of these precious metals reduced the corrosion produced by the burning of the priming. A few makers gained a reputation for the quality of their duelling pistols, among them one Wogdon in whose honour a poem was composed which included the line 'patron of the leaden death'!

Scottish pistols

Early examples of Scottish pistols were fitted with a snaphaunce lock with the unusual feature that, of pairs of pistols, one has its lock fitted on the right-hand side of the stock in the normal way, and the second has the lock on the left-hand side of the stock. During the 17th century the stock was almost straight and fitted with a very long barrel, with characteristic moulding near the muzzle, and a very long thin steel ramrod housed in the stock. Early in the 17th century the pommel was fish-tailed but later became far more heart-shaped. By the end of the 17th century or the early 18th century, the all-metal stock, for by now they were almost invariably completely of metal, was fitted with a heart- or kidney-shaped butt.

Another feature which remained with these pistols right up until their disappearance was the omission of a trigger guard and the use of a small ball trigger similar to that found on some of the early 17th-century pocket pistols. During the second half of the 18th century the heart-shaped pommel was replaced by the so-called ramshorn type which terminated in two inward-curving scrolls. Situated between the two arms was a small ball which could be unscrewed and was the base of a metal needle used to clear the touch hole. The metal stock was frequently engraved with elaborate Celtic scrollwork. Basically the mechanism was the standard flintlock.

Towards the very end of the 18th century and early in the 19th, a number of these Scottish pistols were made

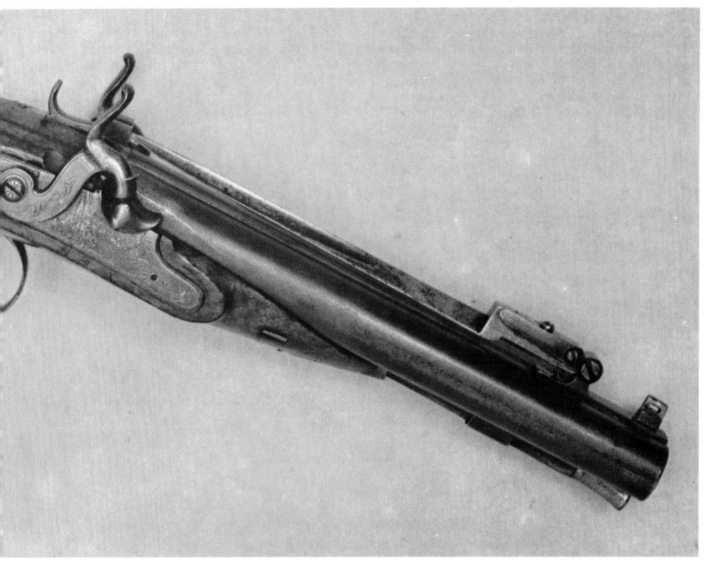

with the characteristic metal stock and thin ramrod; but the butt was of a far more conventional shape, and these are usually known as lobe butts. Birmingham-made versions of these Scottish pistols were issued to some of the Scottish units in the British army, but they were plain, of steel or gunmetal and frequently bear some regimental markings. Scottish pistols are comparatively rare and consequently command high prices.

Continental pistols

In general British firearms were plain and very restrained in the amount of decoration applied, whilst European taste tended more towards the florid. Stocks were generally carved either with patterns or grotesque masks. Inlay of metal, mother-of-pearl and horn was used, although less on pistols than on long arms. The pistol furniture, including trigger guard and side plates, was frequently far more elaborate than on British and American pieces, with high relief and, on more expensive weapons, gilding. Barrels were frequently blued and

gilded or chiselled, as were the lockplates and cocks.

The basic design of the continental weapon does not differ greatly from that of Britain, although there are a few peculiar national features. During the 17th and early 18th centuries the Dutch excelled in carving stocks from ivory, with the butt and pommel shaped in the form of a head. French pistols and those produced in the area of presentday Belgium are often characterised by a form of guard usually described as a pillar trigger guard, on which the rear section is flat and broad, as on the British pistols, but the part in front of the trigger is circular in section. Another common feature of French and Belgian pistols of the same period is of the flat-ended butt, for many swell slightly and then are cut off square. About the same period there was a taste for silver nail decoration on the butt. This applies particularly to weapons of the late 18th and early 19th centuries.

The design of French military firearms greatly influenced the American gunsmiths particularly after the War of Independence (1776–1783), and many of

the American military pistols very closely resemble
those of France, as do their muskets.

One other feature which is very typical of the
continent is the style of casing weapons: the British
case was divided off into sections by straight partitions
whereas the continent favoured a far more elaborate,
but in many ways more satisfactory, method. Each item,
pistol, powder flask, bullet mould etc., was slotted into a
specially contoured section of the case. This ensured a
good fit and a secure hold on pieces, as well as providing
a means of clearly and positively showing if all items

were present. French design also had considerable
influence on the weapons of Russia, for those produced
at the Royal Arsenal of Tula were largely based on
French design books.

Pistols from eastern Europe

The flintlock pistol from the Balkans, including Albania,
Greece, Yugoslavia, Hungary and Turkey in Asia Minor,
again have certain features which distinguish them from
those of western Europe. As a generalisation it can be
said that they are even more decorative than those of
western Europe. The exact identification of these
weapons is by no means certain, and much research
still needs to be done before the provenance of particular
pistols can be given with certainty. However it seems
fairly certain that the very long thin so-called rat-tailed
pistols were largely produced in Albania. They have an
almost straight stock and butt and terminate in an onion-
shaped pommel, but one of their most striking features

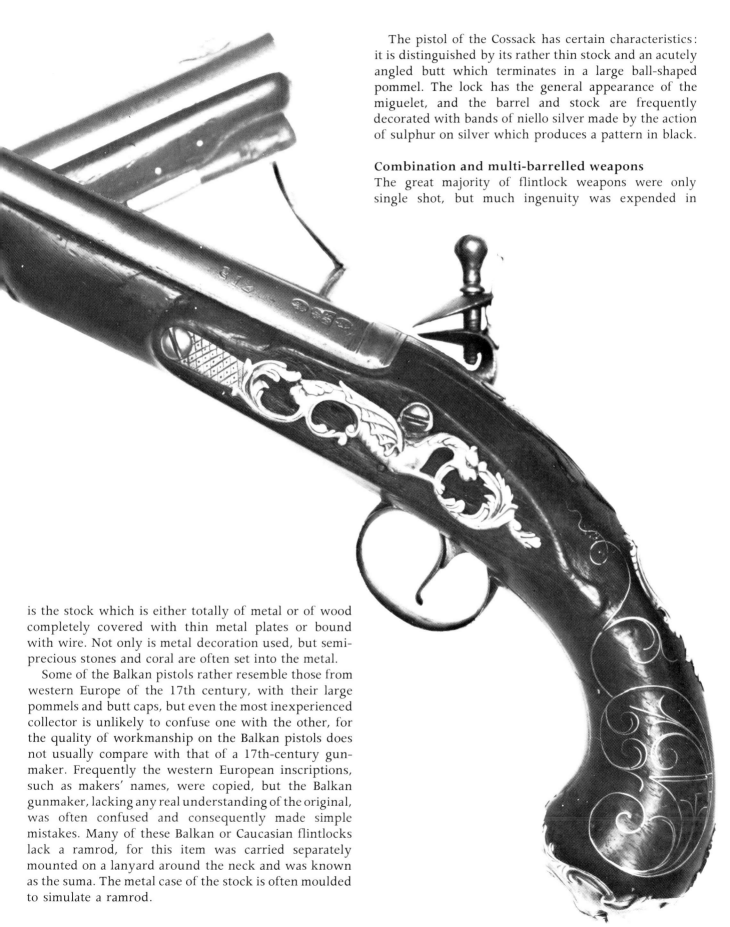

The pistol of the Cossack has certain characteristics: it is distinguished by its rather thin stock and an acutely angled butt which terminates in a large ball-shaped pommel. The lock has the general appearance of the miguelet, and the barrel and stock are frequently decorated with bands of niello silver made by the action of sulphur on silver which produces a pattern in black.

Combination and multi-barrelled weapons

The great majority of flintlock weapons were only single shot, but much ingenuity was expended in

is the stock which is either totally of metal or of wood completely covered with thin metal plates or bound with wire. Not only is metal decoration used, but semi-precious stones and coral are often set into the metal.

Some of the Balkan pistols rather resemble those from western Europe of the 17th century, with their large pommels and butt caps, but even the most inexperienced collector is unlikely to confuse one with the other, for the quality of workmanship on the Balkan pistols does not usually compare with that of a 17th-century gunmaker. Frequently the western European inscriptions, such as makers' names, were copied, but the Balkan gunmaker, lacking any real understanding of the original, was often confused and consequently made simple mistakes. Many of these Balkan or Caucasian flintlocks lack a ramrod, for this item was carried separately mounted on a lanyard around the neck and was known as the suma. The metal case of the stock is often moulded to simulate a ramrod.

33 Pair of Spanish pistols fitted with the usual miguelet locks and belt hooks. Spanish makers frequently marked their barrels and locks with their poinçon, which was a mark impressed into the metal and was often of gold. Royal Scottish Museum, Edinburgh.

34 Spanish musket bearing the date 1720. The lock is chiselled in high relief, and the base areas are gilded, as is the butt plate. A good Spanish-made barrel was highly prized by sportsmen and is often found fitted to a non-Spanish stock. Barrel 34 inches. Bore .64 inch. T. H. Porter collection.

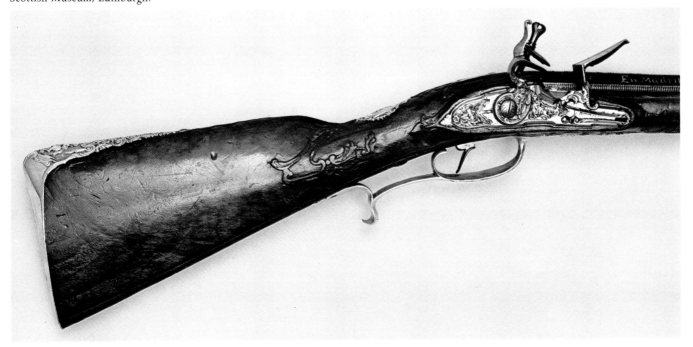

attempting to overcome this severe handicap. Double barrelled weapons were not uncommon, but in addition to these there were more elaborate ones with three or four barrels. With four barrels these were usually arranged in two pairs on a block which could be rotated to bring them into position alternatively. When the first pair had been discharged the block was disengaged and rotated to bring the two unfired barrels into the firing position. Such pistols have some form of catch which has to be unlocked to permit the assembly to be rotated. Pistols using this system were made from the 17th century onwards. Another system using two barrels was the arrangement known as the tap action. Two barrels were fitted, one above the other, to a common breech block in which two small tubes connected each breech to a common pan situated on top of the block. The connecting hole to the lower barrel was interrupted by a round, metal block which, in one position effectively closed the passage from pan to breech, and in another allowed direct access from touch hole to breech. Each barrel was loaded, and the first measure of priming was placed in a recess in the block which was then turned through a right angle, so enclosing the powder within the block and keeping it quite separate from the breech of the lower barrel. A second measure of priming was then placed in the pan, the floor of which was now formed by the edge of the metal block. If the frizzen was then closed, the pistol was ready for firing; when the top barrel had been discharged the block could be turned back, bringing the first load of priming powder into position beneath the frizzen and connecting it to the lower barrel, which could then be fired after closing the frizzen and recocking the action.

Another method of overcoming the single shot limitation of the flintlock was to fit the pistol as part of another weapon. The most commonly found combination is the sword-pistol or pistol-sword. These vary in design but generally consist of a short hunting or riding sword with a barrel mounted just below the cross guard. The trigger is normally housed by the side of the cross guard, and the lock mechanism may be either attached to the barrel or in some way incorporated into the hilt. More rarely will the flintlock be found incorporated in other items, and there are even two or three known examples where pieces of cutlery, a knife or fork, incorporate very small flintlock pistols in their handles. Far more common is the flintlock pistol fitted with a bayonet. Patented in 1781 by John Waters of Birmingham, was the spring-operated bayonet which will be found fitted to pistols and long arms of various kinds. It consists of a bayonet of triangular section, pivoted at the muzzle and operated by a spring so that once the catch, usually positioned on the butt or trigger guard, is released the bayonet will swing forward under the impetus of the spring, to lock into position. Although on the face of it a very useful feature, it was probably rather pointless, for although this type of pistol was recommended by some contemporary writers, no recorded case has so far been located where the bayonet of such a weapon proved of any value in action.

Early long arms
Although pistols are without doubt the most popular of collectable firearms there is also much interest to be found in the collecting of long arms. This term is commonly used by collectors to cover all firearms fired

43

35 Typical Queen Anne pistol with its long, screw-off barrel, high, strongly curved frizzen spring, silver mounts, and gracefully curved butt. It was made by James Freeman of London about 1750.

from the shoulder or from the cheek. Such weapons usually have a long barrel and stock as on a musket, but the term is also used for a variety of other weapons as well. A high proportion of long arms are, of course, military weapons, since these were issued in bulk over long periods.

In the 18th century the flintlock musket of the British Army was the type known as the Brown Bess, but although the use of this term suggests only one weapon there were several variations of the standard musket over the century and a quarter that it was in use. The earliest Brown Bess appeared in the 1720s and was a musket with a large conventional flintlock secured by three screws and housing a wooden ramrod beneath the 46 inch barrel. There were changes in detail until, by the middle of the 18th century, what might be termed the standard Brown Bess musket, the Long Land pattern, had evolved. Its fittings, normally of brass, were a substantial butt plate, trigger guard, pipes and side plate. Later the barrel length was reduced to 42 inches; this model was known as the Short Land pattern. Even this length of barrel was considered by many to be too great, and the question was decided during the Napoleonic wars when demand tended to outstrip the availability of supplies. Looking around for large quantities of readily available flintlock muskets, the government turned to the East India Company, probably the largest private purchaser of weapons, and adopted their pattern Brown Bess which was fitted with a 39 inch barrel. This model, cheaper and easier to produce and therefore more readily available, was known as the India pattern.

The standard pattern Brown Bess musket bears on the lockplate the word 'Tower' with the royal cipher and, up until 1764, a date as well. It is not uncommon to find the name of contractor also engraved on the lock, particularly in the case of privately purchased weapons. Occasionally muskets will be found to bear regimental markings; sometimes the number of the regiment, for at this period all the regiments of the British army were designated by numbers, may be engraved on the barrel, and some indication of ownership may also appear on the butt plate. The India pattern is the most common type available, and because many of these were issued to volunteer units it is not unusual to find the initials of a county, followed by V for 'volunteer' and possibly a number. Since many of the volunteer groups were armed by private subscriptions it is also possible to find military markings appearing on muskets which do not carry the royal cipher or any other indication of Ordnance supervision.

The Brown Bess was fitted with a swivel at the front of the trigger guard and another in the stock near the front ramrod pipe, although it is very unusual to find a musket complete with the sling with which it was carried. British military muskets of the 18th century were almost invariably fitted with a socket bayonet which was also known as a spike bayonet. The blade is short, around 15–17 inches long, triangular in section and fitted by a curved neck to a piece of tube large enough to pass over the muzzle. The short piece of tubing was slotted to fit over a bayonet lug at the muzzle. The bayonet was carried in a leather sheath with brass fittings.

Continental muskets are not dissimilar in general appearance, although there is one feature which almost invariably distinguishes them from the British models. British makers persisted in their method of fixing the musket barrel to the stock by means of the lug and pin method, exactly the same as that used on pistols. The continental gunmakers preferred what was, in many ways, a simpler and more efficient system using barrel bands which slipped over the stock and barrel, whilst near the muzzle was a large nose band which extended some way along the stock.

On the whole the quality of workmanship on military muskets is quite good, but it obviously does not compare with really good civilian work. The weapons are usually serviceable but lack any refinements or frills.

When the percussion system was adopted by the British military in the second quarter of the 19th century, many flintlock muskets were adapted to take the new system. Some Brown Besses were changed to percussion and converted by the pillar and nipple system.

Far less common than the smooth bore military musket is the rifle. The properties of rifling were understood at a very early period, but it was not generally adopted simply on technical grounds. The difficulty of cutting the grooves for rifling on the inside of a barrel with the machinery then available was very considerable. Many of the good quality wheellock sporting guns were fitted with rifled barrels, but the mechanical process, when done by hand, was slow, laborious and very tricky, and consequently the rifle was limited in supply. However the latter part of the 18th century saw the introduction of rifles on a much wider scale. In America there was a type known usually, and erroneously, as the Kentucky rifle. It is characterised by a very long octagonal barrel firing a small-diameter bullet. The stock is slender with a gracefully down-dropping butt and a quite deep-cut shoulder recess. They are frequently decorated with attractive brass inlay, but their outstanding quality was their accuracy. The Kentucky, or to be more accurate, the Pennsylvanian Long Rifle, was undoubtedly a work of art and a weapon which proved itself in sport and war. Another very characteristic feature of the Pennsylvanian Long Rifle was the patchbox set in the butt like those found on wheellock rifles, but the patchbox lid on these rifles was almost invariably of decorated brass. During the American War of

38 Similar to the pistols in plate 49, but much better quality. These pistols, with their holsters, are of silver gilt and probably Turkish. Barrels 12 inches. Bore .65 inch. The Warren collection.

39 Russian flintlock long fowling piece measuring 6 feet overall. The stock is of crossgrained walnut and is carved, whilst the mounts are of silver. On the lock is

TULA and the date 1741. Tula was the chief Russian royal arsenal and produced some very fine quality weapons. Private collection.

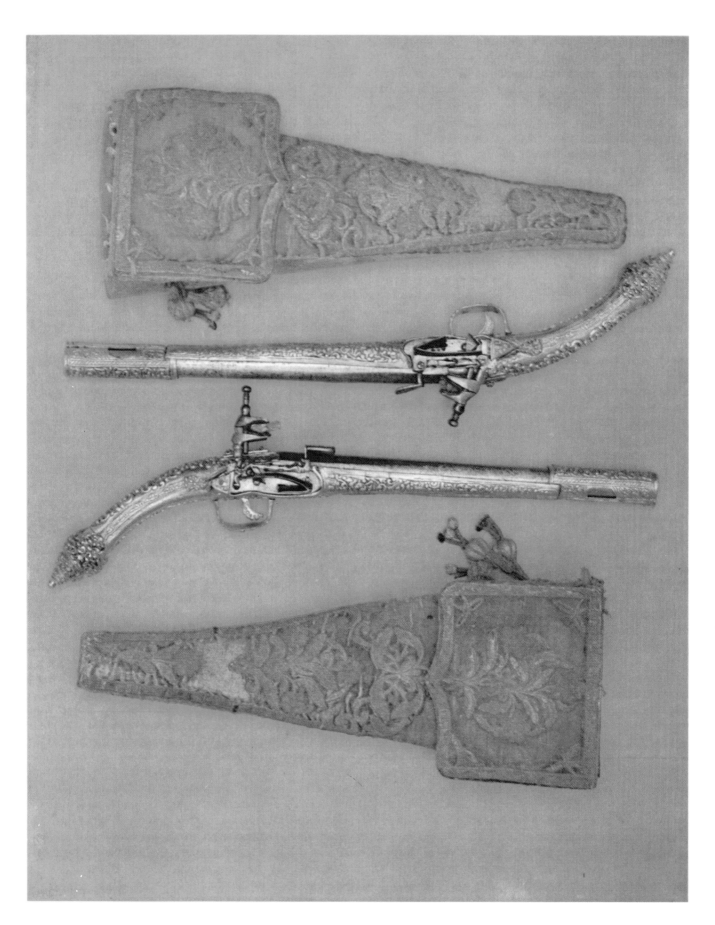

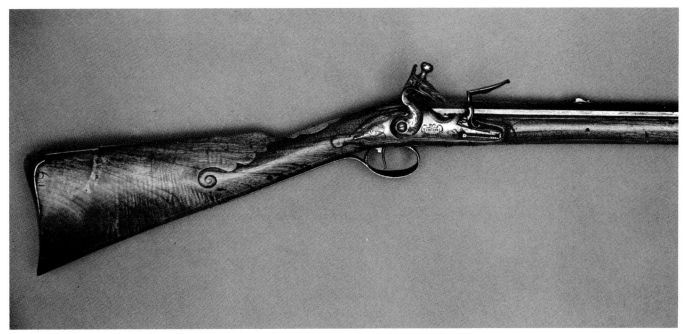

Independence the British army came to know and fear these extremely efficient and accurate weapons, but the British army did not seriously consider adopting a rifle. Captain Patrick Ferguson of the 70th Regiment designed an efficient and very advanced breech-loading flintlock rifle which was issued experimentally on a limited scale to some troops taking part in the American War of Independence. Ferguson himself was killed in 1780 at the Battle of King Mountain, and without his driving enthusiasm to spur on the authorities interest waned: the Ferguson rifle became a sporting weapon and a collector's joy. Only one or two of the military versions are known to exist, but a number of civilian examples are recorded. The breech-loading mechanism was one that was to be used by later gunmakers and consisted of a trigger guard attached to a screwed plug which was removed by rotating the trigger guard. This allowed direct access into the breech from the top of the barrel, so that powder and ball could be placed therein.

Interest in a military rifle lapsed and was not revived until the early part of the 19th century when the winner of a competition to produce a good reliable rifle was Ezekiel Baker. This weapon was adopted by the British government for issue to a Corps of Riflemen which was to be made up of skirmishers trained to act independently and on their own initiative. The Baker rifle with which they were issued was a very sound, if somewhat heavy and cumbersome, weapon. The octagonal barrel fired a ball .625 inches in diameter, and the stock was plain with a brass lidded patchbox in the butt. Unlike the less sophisticated musket the Baker rifle was fitted with sights, and in order that the bayonet should neither obscure nor damage the sights a metal bar was fitted by the side of the barrel near the muzzle. The bayonet, brass hilted and sword-like, was fitted on the bar by the side of the barrel where it in no way interfered with the marksman's aiming.

Blunderbuss

Whereas the rifle was designed to send one bullet to a specific target, the blunderbuss may be described as being precisely the opposite, for it was intended to discharge a number of bullets over a given area. The flintlock blunderbuss enjoyed great popularity with guards on mail coaches and with householders for home defence, as well as being issued in limited numbers to the army and navy. The earlier flintlock weapons commonly have a barrel which appears to be cylindrical but, in fact, has a bore which gradually widens from breech to muzzle. The theory behind the blunderbuss was that a charge of powder would drive bullets along a path determined by the bore, the spread of shot following this line, and the missiles would thus cover a large area. From this idea it follows that the wider the muzzle the greater would be the spread, and some Indian blunderbusses achieve almost grotesque cartoon proportions. In fact, it is now known that the widening, or bell, of the muzzle has only a limited effect on the spread of shot. However, blunderbusses were popular and survive in quantity. Some retain the 17th-century type of barrel which appears externally to be of the same diameter for its whole length, whilst others gradually widen from the breech to the muzzle. A few pistols were made with blunderbuss-type barrels, and these, and the larger weapons, were occasionally fitted with spring-operated bayonets.

British gunmakers produced some very fine quality

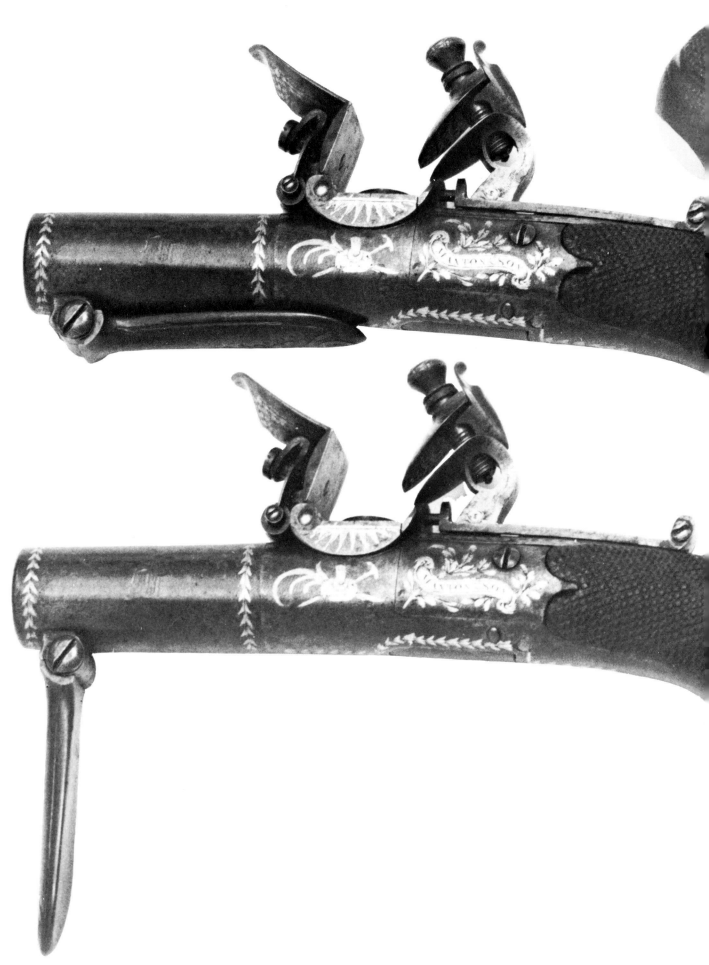

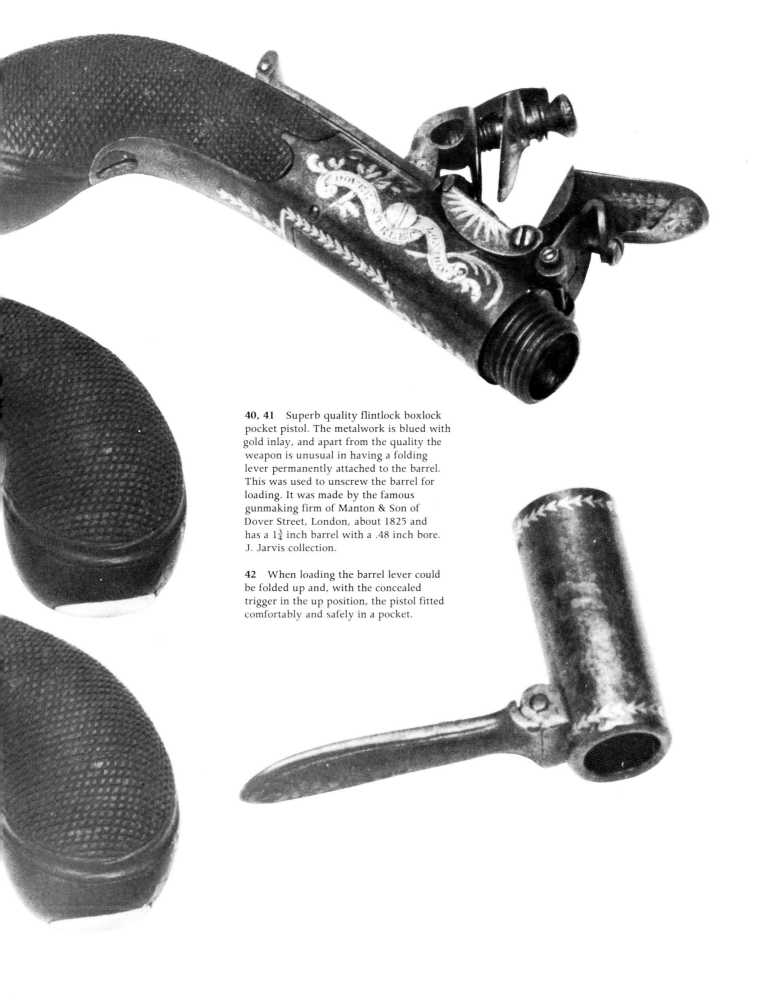

40, 41 Superb quality flintlock boxlock pocket pistol. The metalwork is blued with gold inlay, and apart from the quality the weapon is unusual in having a folding lever permanently attached to the barrel. This was used to unscrew the barrel for loading. It was made by the famous gunmaking firm of Manton & Son of Dover Street, London, about 1825 and has a 1¾ inch barrel with a .48 inch bore. J. Jarvis collection.

42 When loading the barrel lever could be folded up and, with the concealed trigger in the up position, the pistol fitted comfortably and safely in a pocket.

43, 44 Many firearms were combined with a second weapon, as with this sword-pistol by Gandon of London, of about 1760. The shell guard is of silver, as is the inlay. Barrel 3 inches. Bore .45 inch. The Warren collection.

pieces, and, although examples from other countries are known, the blunderbuss seems to have been a particular favourite with the British. The name is usually taken to derive from '*donder busche*', meaning literally 'thunder gun', and certainly the megaphonic effect of the swelling barrel must have been considerable. Those blunderbusses used by mail coach guards are inscribed around the muzzle with the appropriate legend 'For His (or Her) Majesty's Coaches' and a number which indicates the route on which the weapon was carried. Very rarely a Post Office blunderbuss complete with matching pair of pistols may appear on the market, and such a set would be very desirable and in great demand. Two particular varieties of blunderbuss deserve mention, the first being the Indian-made weapon fitted with an exaggerated belling to the muzzle which may well extend to something in the region of four or five inches. They are frequently decorated with brass and mother-of-pearl overlay in squares and shapes on butt and stock. At the other extreme is the small Turkish blunderbuss which is literally a miniature blunderbuss, and although it has the typical shaped shoulder butt it is, in fact, intended to be held in the hand and used as a pistol.

Fowling pieces and sporting guns

Some of the finest quality flintlock long arms were those produced for sporting purposes. During the 17th and early 18th centuries some very, very long barrelled fowling pieces were used; but during the 18th century the length was reduced to a more manageable size, and because of the great popularity of shooting as a sport large numbers of these weapons were made. The quality of workmanship is generally very good indeed, and many of the most famous makers of the country produced examples. The earlier ones are single-barrelled, but from the latter part of the 18th century double barrelled sporting guns were produced. Many of them had the very latest type of lock fitted and incorporated patent innovations of particular gunmakers. Often they had pans which were designed to remain dry even during rain, and others have the pan separate and pivoted so that this can be swung clear of the plate, presumably for easy cleaning and direct access to the touch hole. The barrels of the shotguns often have beautiful patterns in the metal which were produced during their actual construction. The maker's name is usually inscribed on the barrel or along the rib in the case of double barrelled weapons. When the percussion system was introduced in the early 19th century an immediate reaction was simply to modify existing flintlock weapons to take the new system, and all types of flintlock weapons will be found which have been converted to percussion. The commonest system is the pillar and block, but other systems were used. Some gunsmiths merely substituted a hollow-nosed hammer

45, 48 Fine quality cased set of flintlock duelling pistols by Durs Egg, whose trade label is fastened on the inside of the lid of the case. Amongst the accessories is the leather wallet for holding spare flints. The 10 inch barrels are octagonal, and the trigger guard has the spur to assist in a firm steady grip. Bore .52 inch. About 1800. A. J. Galloway collection.

46 Bartolomeo Scalafiotti whose name appears on this pistol is known to have worked in Turin making locks around 1780–1795. The butt is rather larger than is usual in English pistols, and the metal ramrod also differs in detail. Barrel 7 inches. Bore .69 inch. Ed Vaule collection.

47 The characteristic Scottish pistol has

in place of the cock and screwed a nipple into the side of the breech, but others used far more elaborate methods. The general effect of conversion is to reduce the value of a weapon; a flintlock pistol might be worth £100 (US $250), but a similar pistol converted to percussion will certainly not reach this figure. Blunderbusses, duelling pistols, long arms, Brown Besses—all were adapted to take the new system, but after the initial problems of the changeover new weapons were designed around the system and gradually introduced.

Percussion pocket pistols

The mechanical construction of the percussion system was much simpler than that of the flintlock, for there was no need for a frizzen, frizzen spring or adjustable top jaw and cock. All this helped to reduce the cost of production, and Birmingham and Liège became centres for manufacturing large numbers of cheap, but nevertheless quite serviceable, percussion pocket pistols. These normally had slab butts and used a simple boxlock-type of construction with the hammer and nipple mounted centrally above the breech. At one time no collector of any pretentions would even consider these weapons, but so much has the demand increased that today even the simplest of Birmingham percussion pistols is likely to fetch within the region of £10–£20 (US $25–$50).

Percussion pistols

Basically the design of the pistol, apart from the lock, altered very little and percussion versions of all the standard weapons were produced, including duelling pistols. Some of those by continental gunmakers are extremely ornate and very fine examples of their craft. The stocks were frequently of ebony, carved with floral and similar motifs. The large case, with its contoured compartments, enclosed a pair of pistols, two ramrods, small mallet, powder flask, bullet mould and various tools, and the inside is frequently lined with red or blue material. Such sets are much sought after now, although they were at one time rather scorned by the general collector. Military pistols of the period are generally speaking simpler in design than the flintlock variety and will be found to assume fairly large proportions, but as a rule they have a far simpler stock. Many of the British weapons of the mid 19th century are really quite simple with a hook-shaped butt. Barrel

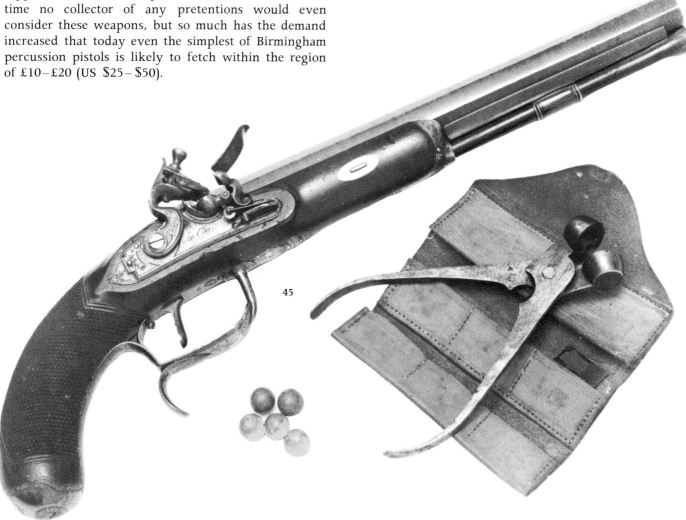

45

inward curling tips to the butt, but later examples evolved to a lobe shape for the butt. The ball trigger was a feature of these weapons, as was a belt hook fitted on the left-hand side of the pistol. Barrel 6 inches. Bore .53 inch. Late 18th century.

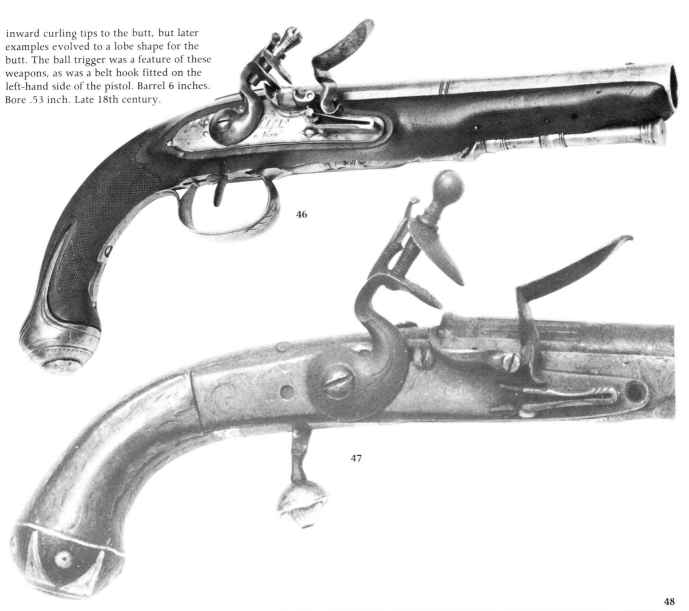

46

47

48

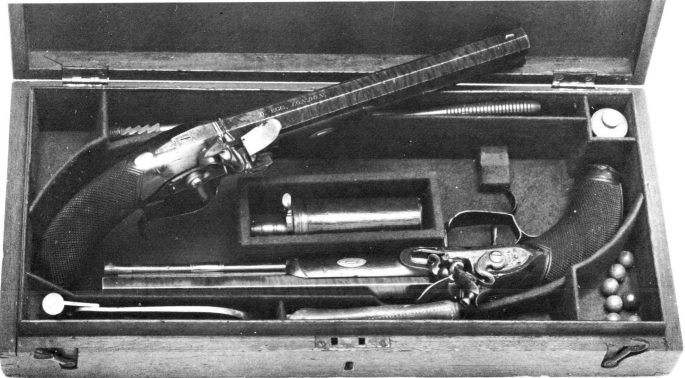

49 Pair of 19th-century, rat-tailed pistols with miguelet locks. They are all metal, being made entirely of brass and steel. This form is usually associated with Albania. Barrel $13\frac{1}{2}$ inches. Bore .58 inch. The Warren collection.

50 Fine quality Austrian flintlock hunting rifle, the lock overlaid with brass and chiselled with typical hunting scenes. About 1740. T. H. Porter collection.

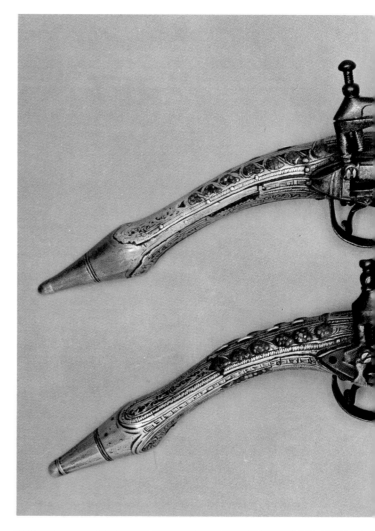

and stock were still held together by bands in the case of continental pistols, but on British weapons this was done either by the pin and lug or by means of a false breech and sliding bar. With this method the barrel terminated in a substantial hook-like projection at the breech end which engaged with a socket cut into a metal block mounted in the stock. To remove the barrel a small, sliding bar, which pierced the stock, usually near the muzzle, was pushed through allowing the muzzle to be raised; the rear hook could then be disengaged from the block, and the barrel could be removed. This system is found on some flintlock pistols as well as on many of the better quality percussion pistols. Scottish pistols were produced fitted with the percussion lock, although they are generally somewhat debased and were costume pieces rather than working weapons.

Later long arms

Many Pennsylvanian rifles were produced with percussion locks, and the majority of available specimens are of the percussion variety. When the British Board of Ordnance were finally convinced of the virtues of the percussion system it began experiments to find an appropriate weapon for the army. Technological development had made it possible to produce rifled barrels faster and more cheaply than previously, and simultaneous experiments were carried out on several different rifles. In 1837 the Brunswick rifle was adopted; in general shape and appearance it was not unlike the Baker rifle, but the method of rifling differed. In place of a series of shallow grooves cut spirally on the inside of the barrel, the Brunswick rifle used two, fairly deep grooves, and a specially shaped bullet with a raised band running around its diameter. This band engaged with the grooves in the barrel, and when fired the bullet was forced to follow their path, so acquiring a spin. This rifle was a little difficult to load, for the raised band on the bullet had to engage with the grooves before being pushed down the barrel. The problem was somewhat reduced by cutting two notches at the muzzle in line with the grooves so making it easier to position the bullet. The Brunswick rifle was not popular with the troops. In 1853 the Enfield rifle, which was of the conventional type with several shallow grooves cut on the inside of the barrel, became the standard weapon. This is quite attractive in its own right, and it is a tribute to its designers and manufacturers that many specimens of this Enfield rifle are still shot by muzzle-loading enthusiasts today.

A number of flintlock blunderbusses were converted to the percussion method, but few were actually made using the new system. Part of the reason for this change was that by the end of the second quarter of the 19th century a new form of personal defence weapon had

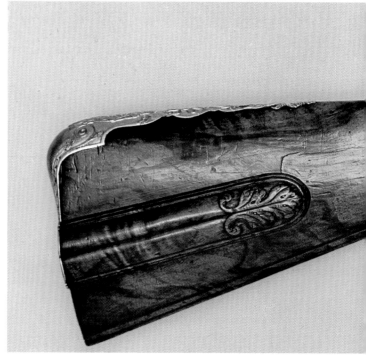

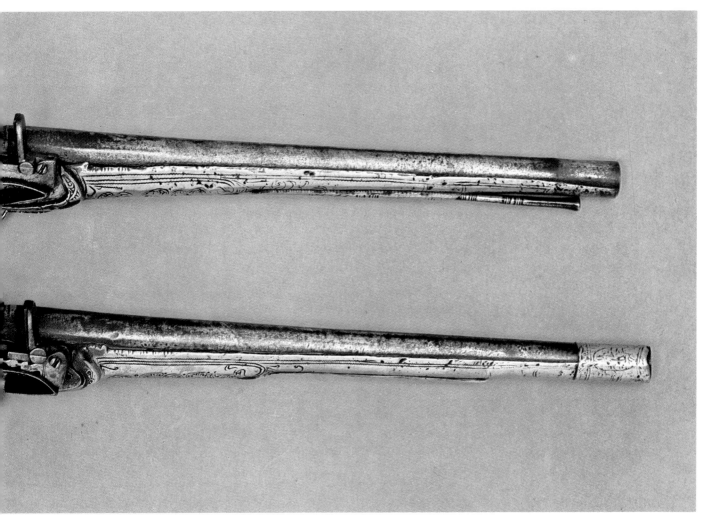

51, 52 Brass barrelled blunderbuss pistol with spring bayonet and side mounted ramrod. The bayonet was locked back under the barrel by engaging the tip with the sliding trigger guard. Made by Waters & Co. in the latter part of the 18th century. Barrel 6¼ inches.

53 Belt hooks are a very common feature of Spanish pistols, and those from Ripoll normally have a ball-shaped termination to the short butt. T. H. Porter collection.

54 This knife-pistol is a similar version of the more expensive types and was probably produced in quantity in Birmingham or Liège. The introduction of reliable revolvers reduced the demand for such weapons. Barrel 4½ inches. Bore .42 inch. Ross Egles collection.

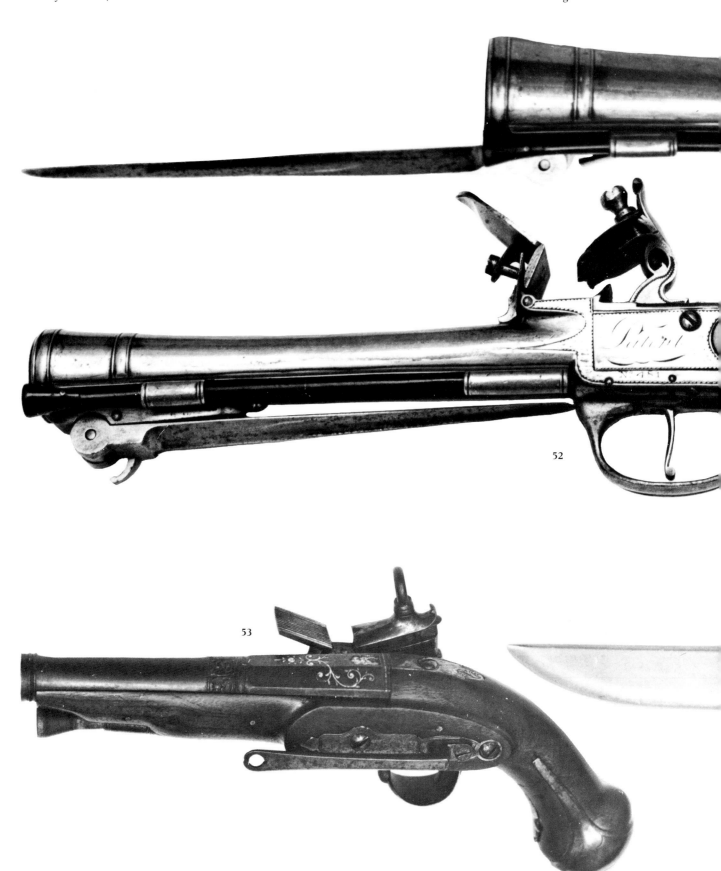

52

53

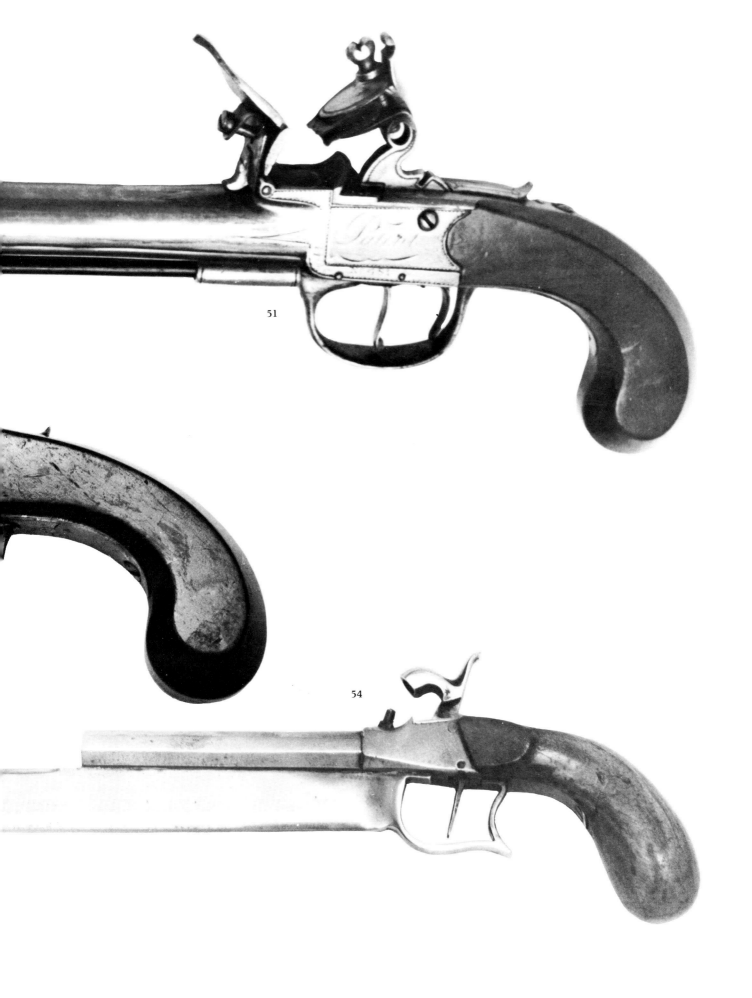

51

54

55 Percussion target pistol with spur on the trigger guard. Made by W. Parker about 1820.

55 Percussion target pistol with spur on the trigger guard. Made by W. Parker about 1820.

56 Double barrelled pistol by John Enty of London, fitted with a top spring bayonet. About 1830. Barrel 8 inches. Bore .577 inch. The Warren collection.

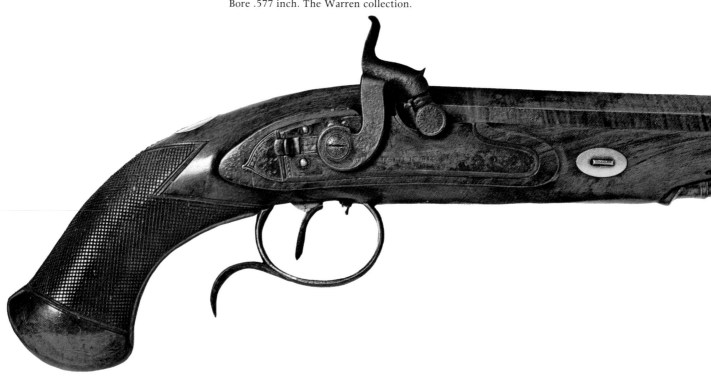

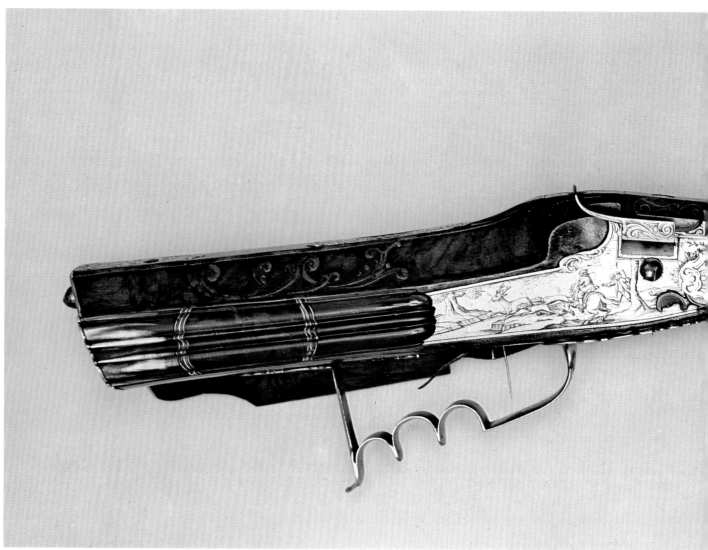

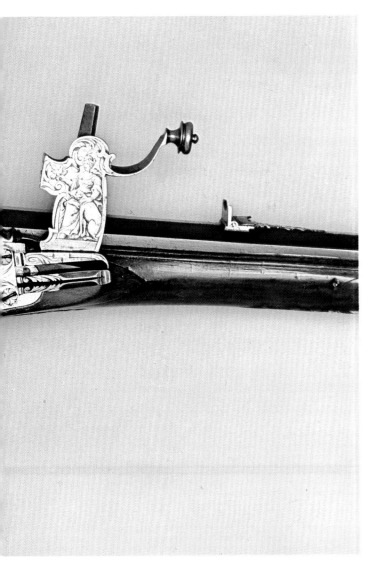

rendered the blunderbuss largely obsolete. The new weapon was the percussion revolver.

Percussion revolver

A revolver would be understood by a collector to be a hand gun which incorporates somewhere in its design a cylinder which holds a number of charges, each of which by one means or another could be fired independently of the others. Matchlock, wheellock and flintlock revolvers were made, but they had shown themselves to be unreliable weapons and for this reason, amongst others, had not previously been very popular. With the simplified ignition system used in the percussion lock gunmakers were soon experimenting with a variety of repeating, revolving weapons. One of the most common was the so-called pepperbox. A solid metal cylinder was drilled with five or six bores, and at the breech end of each a small nipple was fitted. The powder was loaded into one of the bores together with a ball, and a percussion cap was placed upon the appropriate nipple, the process being repeated for each chamber. Pressure on the trigger caused a bar with a solid end to rise slowly until it was an inch or so away from the barrel block when it was automatically released and allowed to fall. It struck the nipple and so discharged the first shot. The trigger was now released and pressure re-applied; this caused the barrel block to rotate to bring a new unfired nipple in line with the hammer ready for firing. Several versions of the pepperbox were made, but most conform to this system. They were very heavy in the barrel, rather clumsy and generally inaccurate but were very suitable for personal defence. The majority of them appear to have been manufactured during the second quarter of the 19th century, but in fact many were by then obsolete, for the true percussion revolver had been developed and perfected by an American whose name has become synonymous with revolvers.

In 1836 this go-ahead Yankee, from Connecticut, Samuel Colt, patented his revolver. It comprised a butt fitted to a frame with a central spigot on to which fitted a cylinder free to rotate when motivated by a very simple reliable mechanism, operated by moving the hammer. To the front of this frame was fitted the barrel, and the whole was locked together in a reasonably secure fashion; this design became known as the open frame system. The earliest types, known as Patterson Colts, are now extremely rare, but the prices that some specimens realised have ensured that the converters and fakers have produced many copies. Despite the undoubted superiority of the weapon, Colt's product was not immediately popular, and he very nearly went bankrupt. However, thanks to an order from the famed Texas Rangers he managed to stay in production, expand and manufacture a whole range of revolvers. Following the Patterson came the heavy .44 revolvers known variously

57 A group of typical English blunderbusses, all with top spring bayonets. *top* Steel barrel, by Richards, about 1800. *centre* Brass barrel, by Jover, about 1780. *bottom* Brass barrel, by Nicholson, about 1800. Elliott & Snowdon.

58 Shooting was always a popular sport and, during the 18th century, was a normal part of a gentleman's life. This detail from the portrait of Mr & Mrs Andrews, painted by Gainsborough in 1750, shows a long fowling piece of good quality with an escutcheon plate on the butt and the barrel fitted with sights. National Gallery, London.

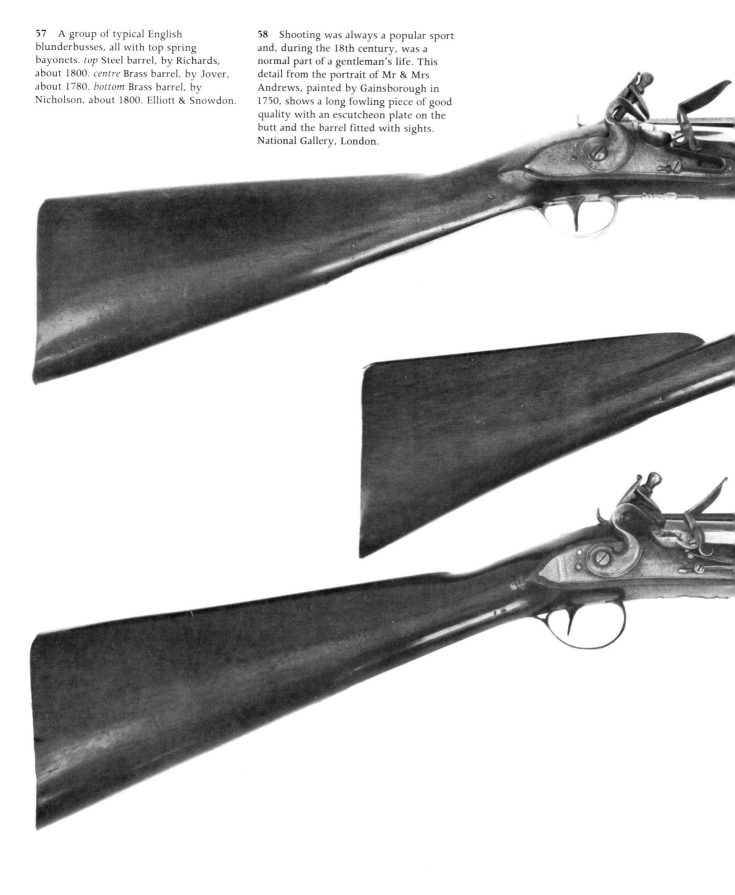

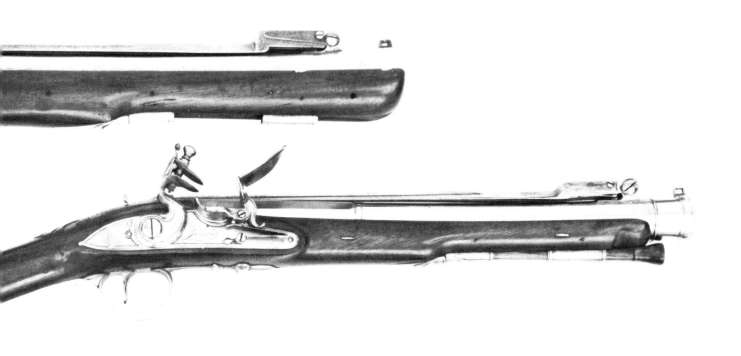

59 Percussion sporting guns by Westley Richards with nicely browned barrels clearly showing the pattern of the metal. The metal flasks were for powder or shot and exhibit just a few of the enormous variety of designs found on such flasks. Barrel 31 inches. Private collection.

60 Butt and lock of a good Pennsylvanian long rifle. It has all the usual features including brass furniture. There is a hair trigger, something not found on all such weapons. It was made by Jacob Dickert of Lancaster, Pennsylvania, about 1775–1780. Barrel 39 inches. Bore .5 inch.

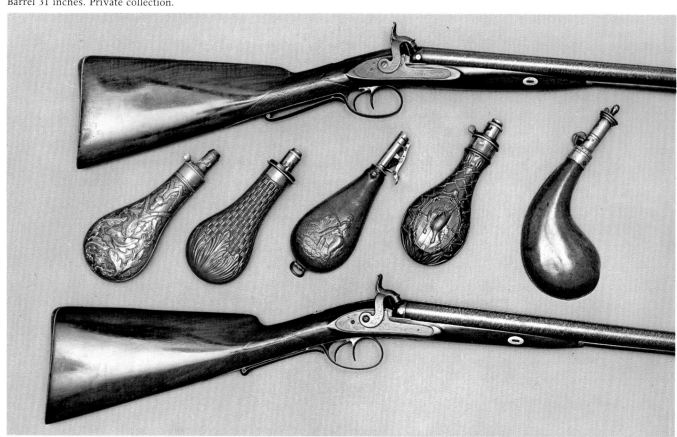

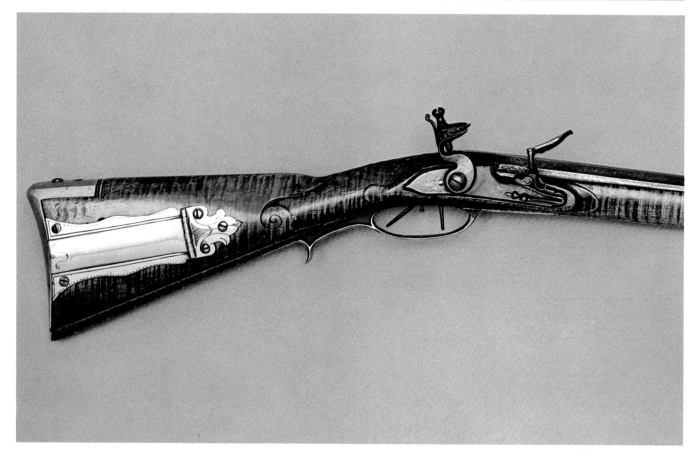

as the Walker, the Whitney and the Dragoon, of which there were several models. He also introduced a smaller pocket revolver in 1847 which fired a bullet of .31 inch diameter. In 1851 Colt put into production what was possibly the most popular of his percussion revolvers, the Navy Model, which fired a .36 inch bullet. In 1861 he followed this up with the Army pattern firing a .44 inch bullet. These three percussion revolvers were to remain immensely popular, and enormous numbers were produced.

Colt opened a London factory in Pimlico near the River Thames and there produced numbers of his pistols. He was encouraged in this project by the response to his display at the Great Exhibition held in London in 1851. However, he aroused a great deal of antagonism, not unnaturally, amongst the British gunmakers; in fact his British venture was not a great success, and his factory was closed. One of the virtues claimed for Colt's revolvers was that, because of his system of manufacture, parts were interchangeable and that for any given model any part supplied from stock would fit. This fact was disputed by the British gunmakers, and at a Board of Inquiry some scorn was cast on his claim. How much of this denigration was inspired by jealousy and by a desire to belittle his product is not certain.

Whilst Colt revolvers were the first to appear on the market in quantity they were by no means the only ones. The 1851 Exhibition showed very clearly that Britain was seriously lagging in this field: the only English maker of any note at that period was Robert Adams. But the impact of Colt's arrival on the scene stimulated the market, and during the 1850s and 1860s large numbers of British percussion revolvers were produced. Possibly the most common were those based on Adams' design whose first model was of the type known as self-cocking. They differed from those of Colt in the method of activating the mechanism; on Colt's revolvers the cylinder was turned and the

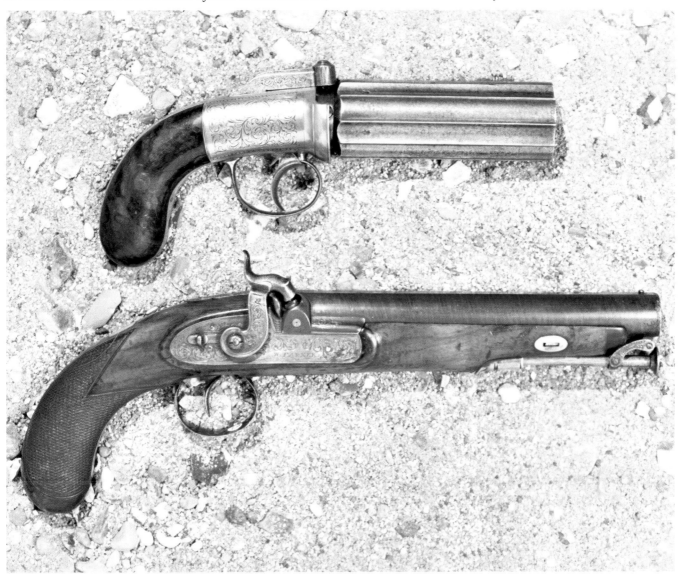

62 Although very typical in some ways, this example of a blunderbuss is rather different in having a short barrel, only 9½ inches long. The butt is full sized so that the weapon was presumably designed for some special purpose. Made by Heylin of London in the late 18th century.

63, 64 Blunderbuss pistol of very good quality made by T. Richards in about 1775. It has simple silver wire inlay decoration on the butt as well as a grotesque butt mask of silver. Unlike many of these weapons the barrel does not unscrew, but it was a muzzle-loading weapon, hence the fitted ramrod.
D. B. Hayden-Wright collection.

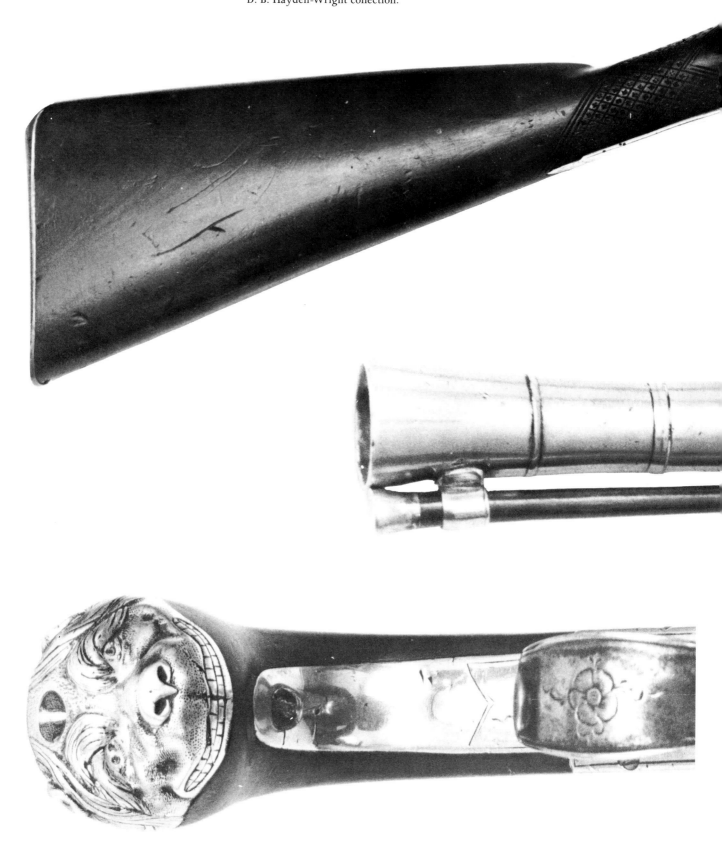

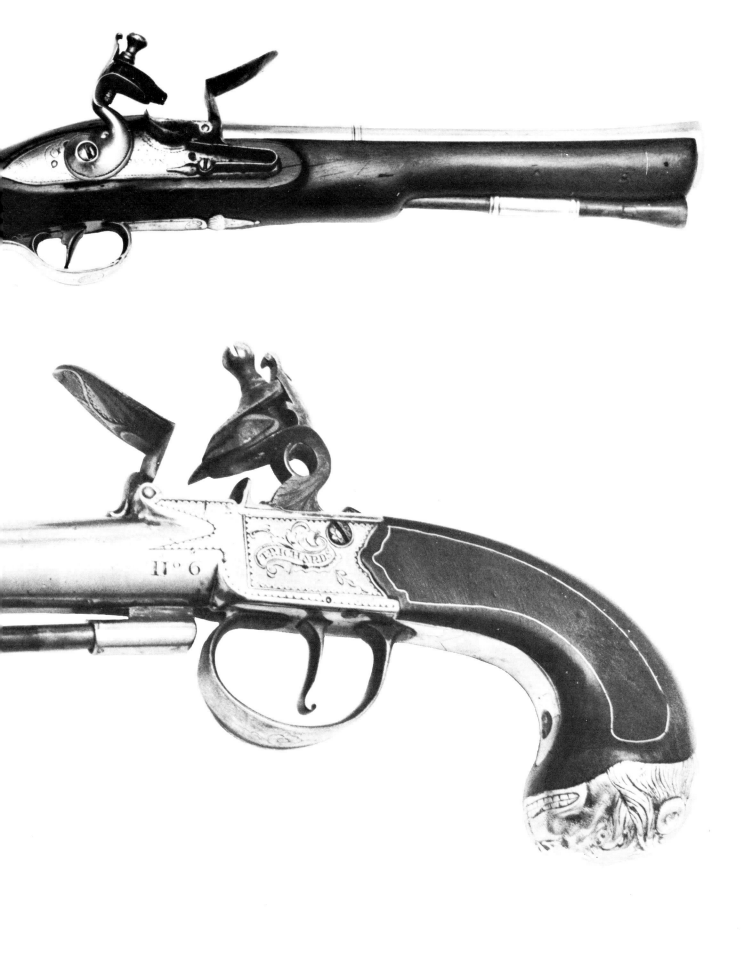

65 *top* Ornately chiselled French 12-bore shotgun of about 1880. *bottom* A most unusual double barrelled 12-bore gun by Stephen Grant of London, fitted with a side spring bayonet. This is a very late example of this form of weapon. T. H. Porter collection.

mainspring placed under tension by pulling back the hammer with the thumb. On Adams' first model revolvers this process was effected by pressure on the trigger, in much the same way as with a pepperbox. Pressure on the trigger caused the hammer to rise and then fall on the nipple as well as rotating the cylinder, and this process could be repeated until all five shots had been fired. Later Adams produced a double action revolver; on this model the hammer could be cocked with the thumb, as on a Colt revolver, but the action could also be motivated by pressing the trigger. Adams revolvers were generally of very fine quality and there are many who argue very strongly that they were superior to Colts.

Adams was by no means the only British manufacturer of percussion revolvers, and Tranter is another name well known to collectors. He produced a variety of models, the earlier ones using his patented double trigger mechanism. In this model the trigger projected through the bottom of the trigger guard, and pressure on this trigger, by the second finger, caused the cylinder to rotate and cocked the action. The hammer was released by pressing a smaller trigger set into the large trigger and housed within the trigger guard. Later Tranter abandoned this method and produced more conventional revolvers with single triggers. Another very famous name was that of Webley, who produced a whole range of percussion revolvers including the very sought-after long-spurred model. The firm of Webley was one of the few to remain in production and continues to

manufacture weapons today.

Numerous patents were taken out to improve the action of revolvers, and the collector of British percussion revolvers has a rich field to explore. The majority of these revolvers were retailed in oak or mahogany boxes, which were usually lined with green baize and divided off by a series of straight partitions, unlike the continental contoured boxes. Although they do vary, the majority of cases hold the revolver, a powder flask, bullet mould and tin of caps, and there is usually a compartment for bullets. These are the basic components, but in addition there may be cleaning rods, screwdrivers, tins of lubricating grease, wads and wad cutters. The inside of the lid usually bears a printed maker's label which should obviously coincide with the name which is to be found engraved along the top of the barrel.

Percussion revolvers constitute a most interesting group of weapons, but those made in England were, until comparatively recently, little sought after. Colt revolvers fetched very high, rather inflated, prices in the auction rooms, whereas equally well made (many would say better) English models fetched comparatively trifling sums. Of late this situation has changed, and a good quality British revolver in fine condition, cased with accessories, can fetch several hundred pounds.

Breech-loading and cartridge weapons

The mid 19th century was a time of great change for firearms designers and producers, and between 1850 and 1890 most of the basic problems involved in pro-

66 Breech-loading pistol by Lepage of
Paris. About 1850. The barrel pivots
sideways to allow access to the breech.
The hammer strikes a pin which passes
through the block to strike the centrefire
detonator of the cartridge. Barrel 8 inches.
Bore .65 inch. The Warren collection.

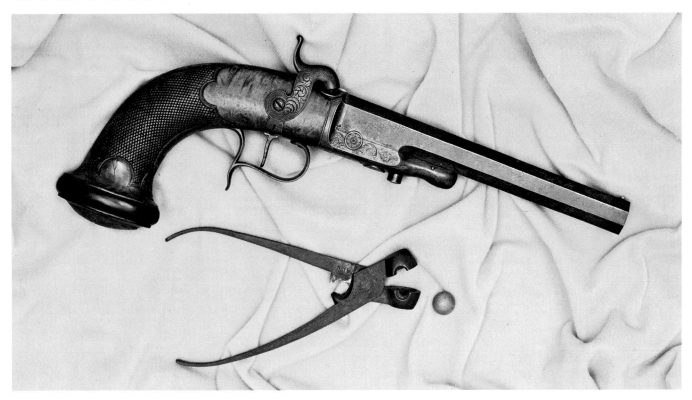

ducing really simple efficient reliable firearms were
largely solved. One of the biggest limitations of the great
majority of matchlock, wheellock, flintlock and percussion weapons was that they were muzzle-loading and
single shot, and that there was a long complicated
loading procedure. Indeed after the battle of Gettysburg
in 1863 it is recorded that some of the rifles picked up
from the battlefields were found to be carrying as many
as ten or fifteen charges, one on top of the other. In the
heat and excitement of battle a misfire had not been
noticed, and the soldier had continued loading, although
in fact the weapon had never been discharged. Methods
of simplifying the procedure had been developed, and
the power horn had been replaced by the paper cartridge.
This was torn or bitten open, a pinch of powder was
placed in the priming pan and the rest poured down
the barrel, the paper serving as a wad which was
hammered down with the bullet. Powder flasks were
still used for many percussion revolvers and duelling
pistols where it was considered important to measure
the charge very carefully.

Much effort had been expended during the whole of
the period from the 14th century onwards in searching
for a means whereby the charge of powder and bullet
could be loaded in from the breech end. This system
offered many advantages: it was a simpler process, the
weapon did not need to be handled quite as much and
it reduced the loss of powder which, when muzzle-
loading, stuck on the inside of the barrel, so reducing
the effective charge. There had been many examples of

breech-loading wheellocks – indeed Henry VIII possessed
breech-loading wheellocks which are still in the Tower
of London. Captain Patrick Ferguson produced a very
practical and serviceable breech-loading rifle, and a
Swiss inventor Johannes Pauly patented another very
effective and reliable breech-loader in 1812. All these
systems had required a degree of technical capability
and skill but, for various reasons, were not taken up
by other gunmakers, so that they remained curiosities.
During this period many systems were developed: in
some the the whole of the barrel moved forward, in
others a chamber was tilted and loaded, as in Hall's
patent. All suffered, to a greater or lesser degree, from
one serious drawback. In order to get access to the
breech there obviously had to be an opening, and unless
this could be sealed very tightly there was an inevitable
loss of gas through it. This meant, quite apart from
discomfort and danger to the shooter, that the firing of
the weapon was likely to be erratic, and the fouling
produced by the explosions sometimes clogged the
action, so rendering the weapon useless.

The solution lay in the production of a cartridge which
could be inserted directly into the breech and would
itself serve to seal the breech and yet allow the case to
be easily withdrawn after it had been fired. Lefaucheux
had produced a system whereby the fulminate was
placed on a separate cap which was incorporated within
a metallic cartridge. Through the side of a metal case,
near the tail, was a small metal rod which touched
against the fulminate cap. When placed in the breech

of the special Lefaucheux firearm a tiny slot was left for this rod to project through the breech. When the hammer fell it drove the rod down to strike the fulminate and detonate it, and the flash within the charge produced a very quick explosion. This system, known as pinfire, was very effective but somewhat limited.

The breakthrough came in 1855 when a Mr Rollin White took out a patent for a breech-loading revolver. This simple and obvious patent merely involved drilling the cylinder right the way through and inserting a small metallic cartridge from the rear end. The cartridges were known as rimfire because the detonating fulminate was deposited on the inside of the edge, or rim, of the cartridge. The solid-nosed hammer struck against the rim, detonated the fulminate and set off the main charge. There were problems in the production of this cartridge, and the firm of Smith & Wesson, who held the patent, started with a small-calibre weapon firing a bullet only .22 inches in diameter. As their skill improved they were able to produce a large calibre bullet of .32 inch, but the principle was now established. Other gunmakers, including Colt, tried to circumvent the Rollin White patent; but it was a master patent, and the principle of the idea was protected. However, this patent expired in 1869, and many other firearms manufacturers were then able to create their own breech-loading firearms.

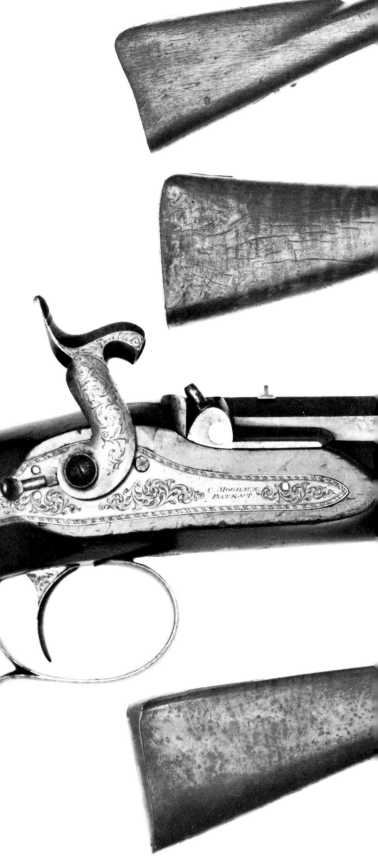

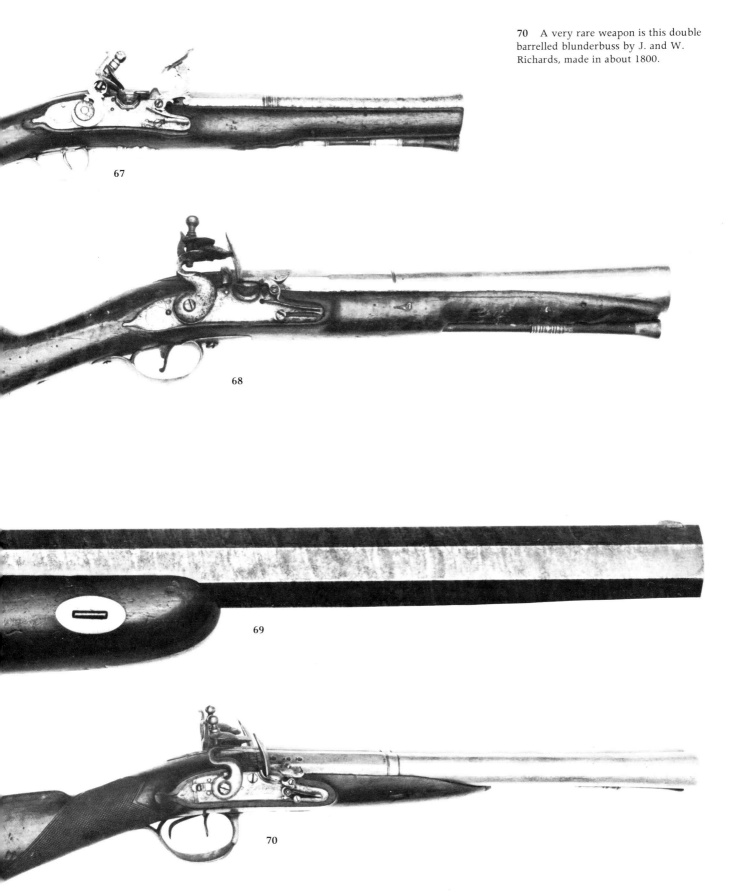

67

68

69

70

71 Cut-away section of a Winchester rifle, model of 1873, clearly showing the under-barrel magazine with its long spring. The Warren collection.

72 Some idea of the great amount of smoke produced by black powder, used in flintlock weapons, can be gained from the firing of this Baker rifle.

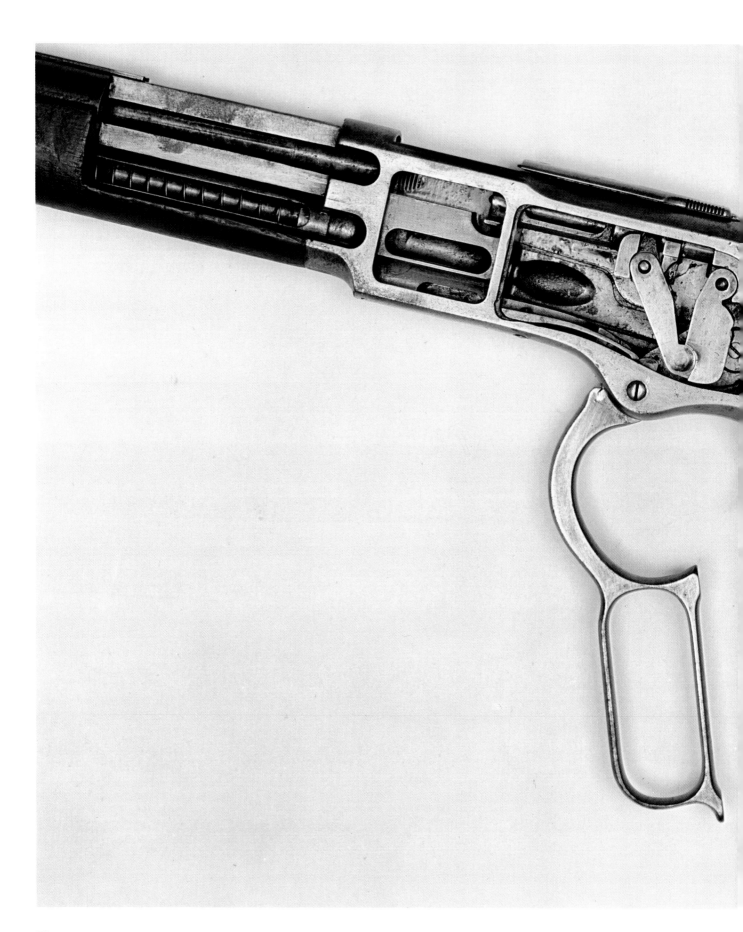

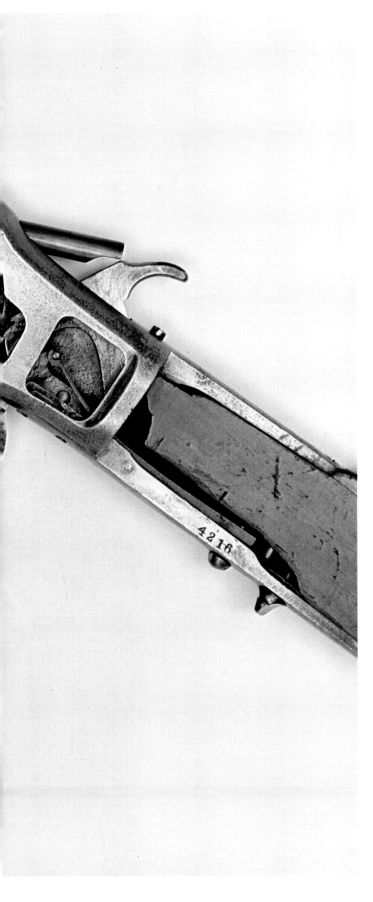

Revolvers could now be loaded quickly and simply, but ejection of the empty case was something of a problem. On early Smith & Wesson revolvers they had to be pushed out using a spigot situated beneath the barrel: the cylinder had to be removed and each case pushed out in turn. It was almost impossible to reload the used cartridge cases, an important consideration for those who were unable to obtain factory-made ammunition easily.

The breech-loading problems having been largely solved, the way was now open to tackle the second problem, that of a more efficient cartridge. The outcome of much experimentation was the centrefire cartridge, the type still used today. In this system the detonating cap is placed at the centre of the base of the cartridge where a pin or hammer strikes it. Early cartridges, such as those used on the Martini Henry rifle of the British army, were not always satisfactory, for the brass cases tended to distort, jam in the breech and split. One by one the technical problems were defeated, and by the third quarter of the 19th century very efficient centrefire cartridges were being produced.

The centrefire cartridge opened the way now to a whole host of new weapons. Bolt-action rifles, repeating rifles and machineguns all became possible. The appearance of the metallic cased cartridge opened the floodgates of invention, and some of the best-known of firearms were produced during this period. In 1873 Colt produced possibly one of the most easily recognised of all revolvers, the Colt Army Single Action. This is beloved by all Western fans, painters and writers, and indeed it often

73 Cased set of rifled percussion duelling or target pistols made by Johann Freund of Suhl. The octagonal barrels bear his name in gold, and the butts are so shaped as to accept the shoulder stock. The mahogany case holds all accessories including mallet, spare nipples, tools and cap dispenser.

74 This French musket is unusual in two respects: its size, only 37½ inches long, suggests that it was made for a boy, and the lock is an uncommon percussion system known as a tube lock.

75 First appearances suggest that this is a conventional sporting gun, but it is an early form of breech-loading weapon, access to the breech being via a side plug which unscrews. Mid 18th century.

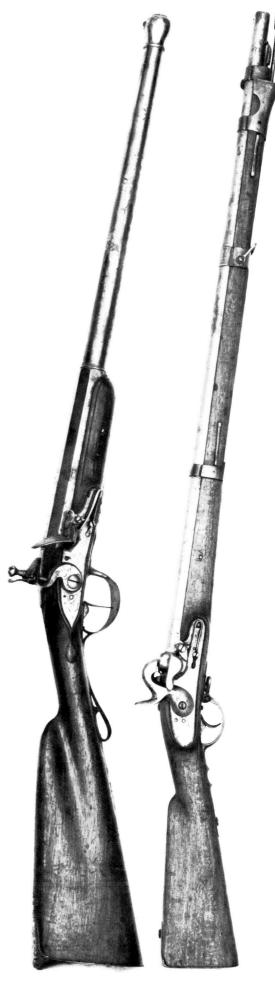

76 American percussion revolvers. *top to bottom* Colt Dragoon revolver firing a .44 inch bullet (1847–1862). Army Colt which also used a .44 inch bullet and which was introduced in 1860. Navy Colt firing a .36 inch bullet and first introduced in 1851. A .36 inch revolver marked 'London Pistol Company' but, in fact, made by the U.S.A. Manhattan Firearms Company. A .31 inch Pocket Colt first introduced in 1849.

77 An 8 shot percussion pepperbox of continental manufacture. Like so many European weapons of this type it has a ring trigger, and later J. Cooper, an English gunmaker, used this form of trigger on his pepperboxes. Many of the continental pepperboxes bear the name 'Mariette'. Barrel 3½ inches. Bore .45 inch. About 1840. D. B. Hayden-Wright collection.

78 English percussion pepperbox revolver of a form typical of the mid 19th century, with usual bar-hammer and furniture. This model is unusual in having an attached bayonet 2½ inches long, a feature rare on such weapons.

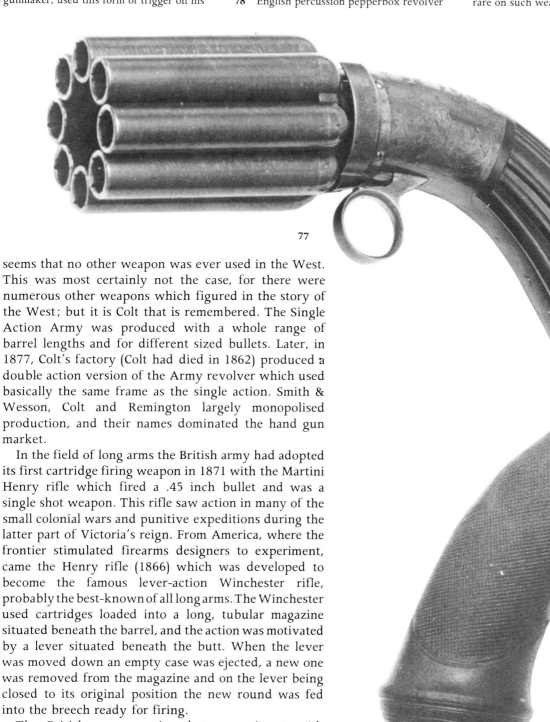

77

seems that no other weapon was ever used in the West. This was most certainly not the case, for there were numerous other weapons which figured in the story of the West; but it is Colt that is remembered. The Single Action Army was produced with a whole range of barrel lengths and for different sized bullets. Later, in 1877, Colt's factory (Colt had died in 1862) produced a double action version of the Army revolver which used basically the same frame as the single action. Smith & Wesson, Colt and Remington largely monopolised production, and their names dominated the hand gun market.

In the field of long arms the British army had adopted its first cartridge firing weapon in 1871 with the Martini Henry rifle which fired a .45 inch bullet and was a single shot weapon. This rifle saw action in many of the small colonial wars and punitive expeditions during the latter part of Victoria's reign. From America, where the frontier stimulated firearms designers to experiment, came the Henry rifle (1866) which was developed to become the famous lever-action Winchester rifle, probably the best-known of all long arms. The Winchester used cartridges loaded into a long, tubular magazine situated beneath the barrel, and the action was motivated by a lever situated beneath the butt. When the lever was moved down an empty case was ejected, a new one was removed from the magazine and on the lever being closed to its original position the new round was fed into the breech ready for firing.

The British army continued to experiment with cartridge weapons, and the final outcome was one of the most famous of all service rifles, the Short Magazine Lee Enfield of 1903, which fired a bullet of .303 inch in diameter. A magazine, situated beneath the breech, could hold 10 rounds. It was a bolt-action rifle and so efficient that it was to see service from 1903 until well after the end of Second World War in 1945. In America similar rifles such as the Krag Jørgensen (1892) and in France the Gras (1874) and Lebel (1886), which were repeating rifles, also used metal cased cartridges.

One remaining major problem still faced the firearms

79 Typical example of single shot percussion pistol made in about 1830–1840. The octagonal barrel is fitted with a swivel ramrod. The quality is fairly good, and the action has a sliding safety catch set behind the cock. Barrel 9½ inches. Bore .5 inch. Marked on the top of the barrel 'Moore & Son'.

80 A so-called transition revolver; these were little more than a shortened pepperbox with a detachable barrel fitted. This example is a little unusual in having a long spurred hammer instead of the more usual bar-hammer. Barrel 5½ inches. Bore .47 inch. G. Kellam collection.

78

79

80

81 Pocket pistols of the late 18th century. *top* By T. Ketland with a $2\frac{7}{8}$ inch barrel and .4 inch bore. *bottom* By W. Parker with a 1.5 inch barrel and .4 inch bore. This one is fitted with a folding trigger which only springs down when the action is cocked.

82 The result of 500 years of firearms is a weapon such as this Remington Model 1100 Auto. It is produced in a variety of sizes and can take three or five shots depending on the gauge. Gowers collection.

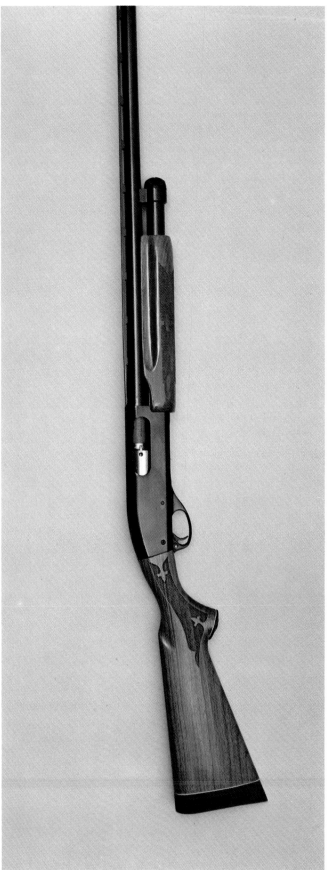

83 Detail of the barrel of the Tranter revolver (84).

84 English double trigger Tranter percussion revolver in an oak case with all the accessories including a bullet mould. This fine example is of special interest

since it bears the address of A. B. Griswold of New Orleans. A number of these weapons saw service in the American Civil War. J. Jarvis collection.

designers: there was the challenge of producing a firearm which, once activated, would fire continuously – what is today known as a machinegun. Experiments were made by Sir Hiram Maxim, who argued that, since for each action there is an equal and opposite reaction, some of this reactive energy could be used to activate the mechanism of a gun. The action would eject the empty case, withdraw a new one from a magazine, insert it into the breech, fire it and repeat the sequence until either the ammunition was exhausted or the mechanism was stopped externally. Maxim devoted a great amount of energy to the problem, and the outcome was the Maxim machinegun of 1883, which was later taken up by a large number of European armies. The Germans adopted it, and the British slightly modified the system and produced the Vickers Maxim which was essentially the same weapon. The magazine on these weapons was not fixed but consisted of a canvas belt with cartridges spaced along it. Once the idea had been pioneered, numerous other systems were produced. Military thinking was at first rather slow in accepting this terrible new weapon, but by the time of the tremendous conflict known as the First World War (1914–1918) the machinegun was an established weapon which did tremendous execution on both sides.

It was apparent to firearms designers that this principle of self-loading could be applied to hand firearms, and so they began to experiment. The first really practical self-loading pistol was produced by Borchardt in 1893 and consisted of a complicated mechanism involving a coil spring and a rather tricky toggle action. The system proved, however, to be basically sound: it was modified and simplified by George Luger, and in 1898 the famous Luger automatic pistol appeared, which saw service with the German army through the whole of the First World War and much of the Second. Soon a crop of other pistols appeared including, in 1911, the Colt automatic, which has had a tremendously long active life and indeed is still used today.

Firearms development did not cease with the production of self-loading pistols but continues today with attempts to improve the propellent and the bullet. A most important innovation was the introduction of smokeless powders. From early in the 14th century up until the mid 19th, battlefields were partially obscured by clouds of smoke produced by the burning gunpowder. In the 1890s the first of the smokeless powders was produced, and for the first time commanders were able to see their troops reasonably clearly without having to wait for the clouds to disperse.

There was a great deal of experimentation on the ideal size of bullet, and the modern trend is towards a small calibre, as small as the .22 inch size normally associated only with sport and target shooting. There

85 A new model Remington Army single action percussion revolver in very fine condition. These revolvers of 1861 fired a bullet .44 inch in diameter which was forced home with the pivotted lever secured below the 6 inch barrel. J. Jarvis collection.

86 Double action percussion revolver made by J. M. Cooper of Philadelphia about 1865. It fired a .31 inch bullet and has a general resemblance to the Colt revolver in appearance, but the position of the trigger indicates that it is not a single action mechanism. Barrel 4 inches. G. Kellam collection.

87 Double action percussion revolver made by the London Armoury about 1860. It is of a type patented by James Kerr in 1858–1859 and was intended to offer a revolver which was simple enough to be easily maintained by any competent armourer or smith. S. Durrant collection.

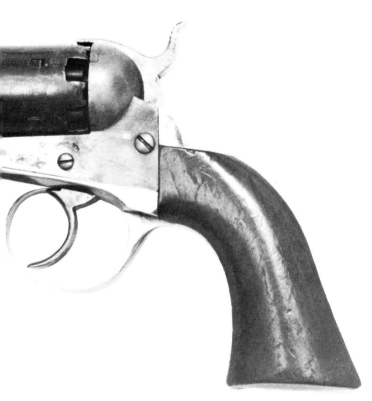

is, too, much research being undertaken into the ideal shape and size of cartridge.

One development, which was started prior to the First World War and has continued ever since, was in the use of automatic rifles. Generally the machinegun was a heavy weapon designed to provide long and continuous fire, but some farsighted military planners saw a need for a repeating rifle which could supply short bursts of rapid fire. One of the first effective models was designed by a Mexican, made in Switzerland and used by the Germans; it was known as the Mondragon. During the First World War the B.A.R., the Browning Automatic Rifle, was developed, and in 1921 the Thompson sub-machinegun, the famous Tommy gun, was produced. It was known as a sub-machinegun largely because it used pistol ammunition, in this case .45 inch.

During the Second World War the Germans experimented extensively with automatic rifles, and in 1942 they produced the M.Kb.42, which was a repeating rifle firing a short 7.92 mm. cartridge and which used a mechanism operated by blowback. Some of the gases produced by the explosion were tapped off and used to drive a breech block back to the cocked position, where it was impelled forward by a spring to fire the next cartridge, the whole process being repeated until the trigger was released or the ammunition ran out. In 1944 they changed the designation of this weapon from the machine pistol to the Sturmgewehr, which means literally 'assault rifle', and this firearm set the pattern for future development. Following the Second World War the Russians probably led the field and eventually came up with the AK 47, produced in 1947, which has proved to be one of the most successful assault rifles. This has been followed by the FAL, the FN and the Armalite series of weapons, all of which are in use by some force or other throughout the world today.

Collecting breech-loading and cartridge weapons
The collector wishing to specialise in cartridge and breech-loading weapons encounters certain peculiar problems. Most of the Western democracies accept an antique as being more than a hundred years old. This is a loose but workable definition, and in Britain the police and customs accept that any firearm which uses any system of ignition up to and including the percussion is an antique, and therefore at the time of writing (August 1973) weapons using these systems require no form of licence or permit. However the 1860s and 1870s saw a number of cartridge breech-loading weapons introduced, and this situation has brought about a conflict of views. Can a cartridge weapon, such as the 1873 Single Action Army Colt, be an antique? The interpretation of this problem has produced some peculiar and rather bizarre results, where some constabularies claim pinfire weapons are not antiques, and others accept them as such. In

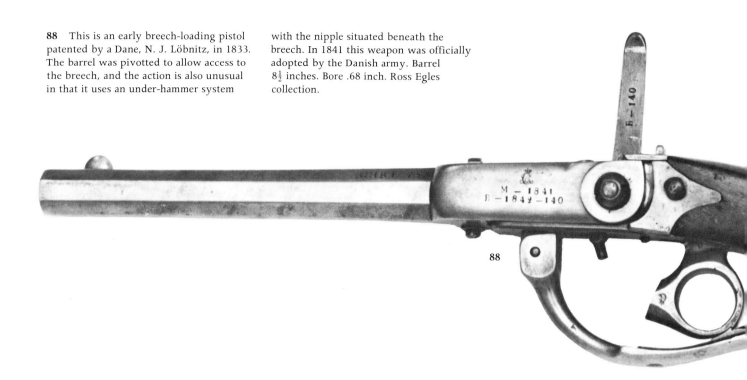

88 This is an early breech-loading pistol patented by a Dane, N. J. Löbnitz, in 1833. The barrel was pivotted to allow access to the breech, and the action is also unusual in that it uses an under-hammer system with the nipple situated beneath the breech. In 1841 this weapon was officially adopted by the Danish army. Barrel 8½ inches. Bore .68 inch. Ross Egles collection.

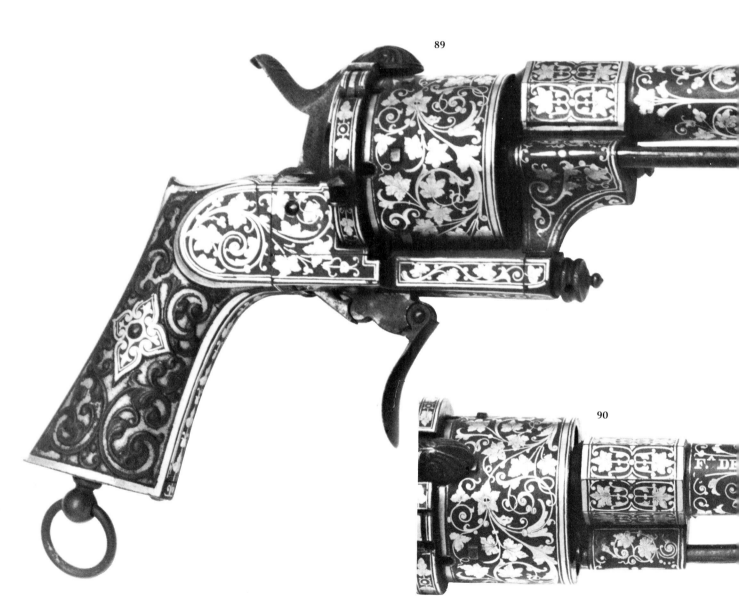

89 Pinfire revolver with folding trigger and a lanyard ring on the butt. It has been embellished with inlaid gold decoration overall. The rod below the barrel was used to push empty cases out of the cylinder. Elliott & Snowden.

90 Detail of the barrel of the pinfire revolver (89) showing the name of the maker who worked in the famous Spanish gunmaking town of Eibar.

91 Detail of the Löbnitz pistol (88). In the open position the charge is placed directly into the breech.

91

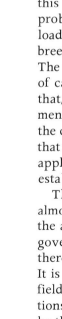

Britain the whole question has been thrown into a ferment by the appearance of a Government document known as the Green Paper Cmnd 5297 which contains certain proposals governing the collecting of firearms and also attempts to define an antique firearm. The yardstick taken is that any weapon which uses a self-contained cartridge incorporating primer, explosive and bullet shall not count as an antique. At first glance this seems reasonable, but in fact it does raise certain problems: under this definition Henry VIII's breech-loading wheellock may not be an antique. Does Pauly's breech-loading shotgun of 1812 fall within this category? The Green Paper also suggests that, in future, collecting of cartridge weapons should be prohibited. It is likely that, as a result of strong representations, the Government have given further consideration to the position of the collector of modern weapons. It now seems probable that the collecting of such weapons may be allowed if the applicant can provide very satisfactory credentials and establish a bona fide interest.

The position in other countries differs, although almost every government places some restriction on the acquisition of modern weapons. The most liberal of governments is to be found in the USA, but even here there are some restrictions on certain types of weapons. It is therefore as well for any collector considering this field to check very carefully on regulations and restrictions imposed by law. It is a great pity that there should be this problem, for the period particularly up until the 1920s was one when there was tremendous experimentation in all forms of rifles and pistols, all of which are worthy of study. One further point must be borne in mind: in Britain antique firearms may be kept without the need to hold any form of licence. Should the collector wish to fire the weapons, however, the situation changes, and a Firearms Certificate is required, as well as a permit to purchase black powder.

92 For the enthusiast there is a special attraction in using his antique firearm. The necessities are many and include powder flasks, grease, percussion caps, tools, ramrods and carefully cast bullets.

93 The variety of projectiles used over the centuries is enormous, and this selection covers but a few. T. H. Porter collection.

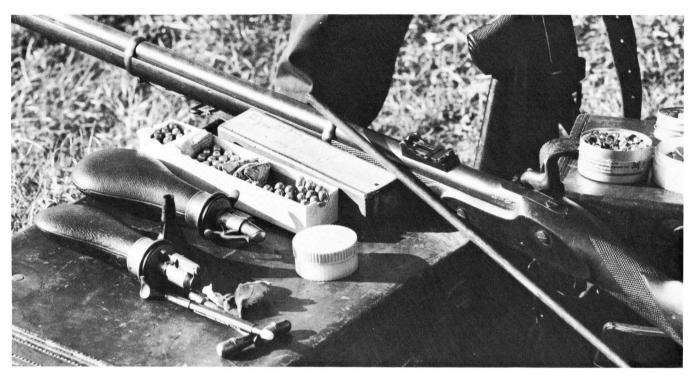

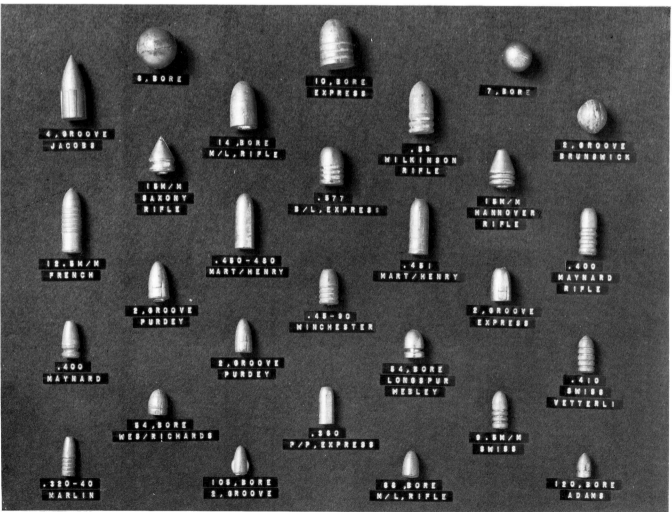

4,GROOVE JACOBS

8,BORE

10,BORE EXPRESS

7,BORE

14,BORE M/L,RIFLE

.58 WILKINSON RIFLE

2,GROOVE BRUNSWICK

18M/M SAXONY RIFLE

.577 B/L,EXPRESS

18M/M HANNOVER RIFLE

12.8M/M FRENCH

.450-480 MART/HENRY

.451 MART/HENRY

.400 MAYNARD RIFLE

2,GROOVE PURDEY

.45-90 WINCHESTER

2,GROOVE EXPRESS

.400 MAYNARD

2,GROOVE PURDEY

54,BORE LONGSPUR WEBLEY

.410 SWISS VETTERLI

54,BORE WES/RICHARDS

.360 P/P,EXPRESS

9.8M/M SWISS

.320-40 MARLIN

105,BORE 2,GROOVE

58,BORE M/L,RIFLE

120,BORE ADAMS

How to record and research the collection

Thirty years ago the danger of purchasing a forged antique firearm was negligible, but unfortunately the risk has steadily increased until today it is ever present. When demand was small the available supply was more than adequate, and it was not worth the forger's time and trouble to produce a good fake. Rising demand is now chasing a diminishing supply, and yesterday's rubbish can be today's bargain, so that the prudent collector will want to assure himself of a piece's authenticity.

It is important to decide one point before any purchase is made, and that is, how much restoration one is prepared to accept. Ideally the answer will be 'none at all', but it is not always possible to adhere to this ideal, and compromise is necessary. Practically the best answer is probably 'as little as possible', and this acceptable amount will depend on the weapon's rarity, price, condition and quality of restoration. Work carried out by an expert restorer is virtually indistinguishable from the original, but, alas, some restorers are less fastidious or less capable.

The question of value has already been discussed, but it is worth repeating that each item is worth precisely what a collector will pay. What one has to decide is whether the item seems to be worth that amount, and the authenticity of the item is obviously a most important consideration. Experience is of prime importance, and this is something which comes slowly; but some suggestions can be offered.

The 'feel' of a weapon is impossible to describe but is nevertheless a tangible fact, as any collector of standing will verify. The pistol or long arm should feel comfortable and sit firmly in the hand or at the shoulder, and if a weapon feels top heavy or somehow uncomfortable it warrants a closer look; this is particularly true of top quality pieces.

A close examination should now be made of the whole weapon with particular attention being paid to the fitting of the metalwork into the stock or butt. Each piece should sit exactly into the wood with only a minimal space which does sometimes develop through shrinkage or bruising. Any signs of cutting away, building up or any repair should be given a close scrutiny. It is only very rarely that a part of one weapon fits exactly into place on another, and some filing or cutting is usually required; this is particularly true of the lock on a flint or percussion weapon. Repairs on the stock do not necessarily condemn a piece as suspect, for repairs were made to weapons during their working life, a point to be borne in mind.

Obviously the parts of the weapon should be consistent as far as period is concerned, and an early 18th-century flintlock pistol with a lock incorporating a roller on the frizzen would suggest that something is very much amiss. The maker's name and proof marks will help in dating a weapon, and again these should be in keeping with the other features including the method of construction.

Rust is a prime enemy of the collector of firearms, but it does have a very limited use, for it may help to authenticate a piece. If the furniture of the weapon is of steel, then obviously the degree of rusting on furniture, barrel and lock should be roughly the same. If there are big differences can these be explained? It may happen that a pistol is kept in a case which has become damp and has therefore caused heavy rusting wherever the metal is in contact with the case. If the metal is blued, the colour should be looked at, for the original blue has a characteristic light, almost shiny quality about it which is difficult to achieve with modern preparations. If possible the lock should be removed and the mechanism checked: it has been known for rubber bands and blocks to serve as makeshift springs.

Dedicatory inscriptions, coats of arms and owner's names engraved on the firearms should always be treated with great caution unless there is some contributory supporting evidence.

Cased sets are always desirable, but each item should be examined to see if it is really part of the set, for it is now easy to acquire reproduction flasks, bullet moulds, cap tins and other items.

Kits are available now to build a Kentucky rifle, a blunderbuss, a Brown Bess, a Queen Anne pocket pistol and a Scottish pistol. There can be no objections to such kits if the finished product clearly shows that it is indeed modern. The trouble arises when these have been well made and are then distressed and offered as genuine antiques. Again the only real safeguard is experience or an unequivocal declaration by the vendor that the piece is genuine. Failure to obtain such a guarantee may well give rise to some doubt on the part of the purchaser.

So far percussion revolvers, with the exception of Colts, seem to have escaped the serious attentions of the forger. The main parts of Colt's firearms were individually numbered, and a good example should have matching numbers on all components. However, if this is not the case it does not necessarily mean that the weapon is suspect, for one of Colt's big selling points was the interchangeability of parts. It is therefore quite feasible that the particular weapon may have had a part replaced during its working life; but those with matching numbers are more highly regarded than others, and there have been attempts made to alter numbers.

The problem has been further complicated by the appearance on the market of facsimile shooting weapons. Navy, Army and Dragoon Colts and Remingtons have all been reproduced and are clearly marked as being modern weapons. In Britain, since they are intended as weapons to be fired, a firearms certificate is necessary before one can be acquired. It is therefore unlikely that British collectors will be seriously concerned with this problem, for once such a pistol has been placed on a firearms certificate it is not an easy matter to have it taken off, but this situation does not necessarily apply in other countries. The markings indicating its modern origin may well be obscured by distressing or similar processes. The greatest risk lies with the rarer Colt revolvers, for so high have their prices risen that the forger now finds it worthwhile to undertake quite elaborate reconstruction of specimens. In many cases dealers who specialise in these items are having them X-rayed so that welds and modifications will show up.

British percussion revolvers do not, as yet, seem to have attracted the attention of the faker, apart from some cannibalisation where cylinders are swopped and springs replaced. The most likely modification to be found on these weapons is that they have been reblued.

The problem of reblueing is very relevant to modern firearms, since their value is reduced if this has been done. A collector must decide if it is better to acquire an example in reasonable, although not original, condition rather than not have a specimen at all.

From about 1860 onwards the number of patents taken out in the field of firearms was very high, and it is important to have some knowledge of the development of firearms, for there were so many varieties and oddities that it is advantageous to be able to recognise them, since some are extremely scarce. With modern firearms the numbering is of great importance, but fortunately in the case of many of the better-known firearms such as Lugers, Colts and Smith & Wessons, the numbers used for the various years are known, and reference can be made to the appropriate books to identify the precise model and date of manufacture. Superficially the many modern firearms all look identical, but there are numerous minor variations; some are much rarer than others, and it is essential to have some really reliable reference source by which these matters may be checked.

Many of the problems of buying antique firearms are considerably reduced if one deals with a reputable dealer or auction room, where one has some guarantee of reliability. A dealer should be prepared to back his judgement and reputation by giving a guarantee of authenticity, and he should also point out any defects that he knows of. However, in the final event it is still up to the collector to make up his own mind. There are few collectors who can claim never to have made a mistake, and the best that one can hope for is that the mistakes will be few and inexpensive.

Stripping and recording a weapon

Having acquired a new item for the collection, one of the first jobs to be undertaken should be the full recording of the weapon, and this is best done by stripping the whole piece to its basic components. This may seem an unnecessary complication, but the time spent on cleaning, repairs and recording when the weapon is first acquired can save trouble later on. It is always worth checking that the weapon is not loaded: if it has come through the hands of a dealer he has probably done this, but check in any case. A piece of dowelling can be pushed down the barrel until it is stopped and the muzzle position marked. The dowelling is then withdrawn and laid along the top of the barrel: if it extends the full length right to the rear, then it is reasonably safe to assume that there is nothing in the barrel. If the dowelling indicates that there is a solid inch at the breech take care, for it may mean that a charge and ball are still in position. In this case the best thing to do is to use a jag, a screw fixed to the end of a metal rod. This can be pushed down the barrel to engage with the ball, which can then be withdrawn and the powder shaken out. It cannot be stressed too strongly that gunpowder, although losing some of its potency over the years, is always explosive and should be treated with care.

The stripping of a wheellock obviously requires a degree of skill, and since these are comparatively rare and very expensive it is not suggested that their dismantling should be lightly undertaken. A flintlock presents few basic problems, the first step being to remove the lock: undo the screws which pass through the stock from the side plate. Here it must be stressed that one of the most important considerations is the use of a correct size of screwdriver. This may necessitate the purchase of several different sizes; it may even mean filing down standard ones, but the time and trouble spent will be more than amply repaid. The wrong size of screwdriver tends to fracture the heads of screws, or it can so easily slip and score the woodwork, thus

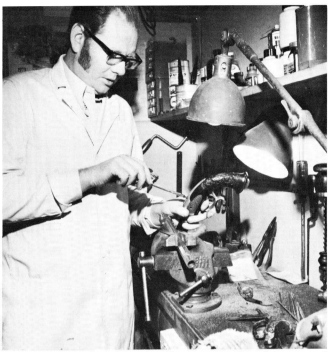

reducing the value and pleasure of possession. If the screws refuse to move there are several remedies which may be tried; often some penetrating oil, applied to the screws where they engage with the lockplate, and left for a while, will be sufficient to loosen them. If this fails, then very gentle and careful tapping with the screwdriver can be tried. If the screw is conveniently placed, then a heated screwdriver placed on it may cause it to expand sufficiently to loosen it, but great care is necessary to avoid damage to the woodwork. If all other methods fail the last desperate remedy is to drill out the screw, but this is not a course to be recommended. If the piece is found to be so welded in by rust and dirt, it is probably well worth while consulting a qualified gunsmith. Fortunately it will be found that most screws will unscrew, and the lock can then be removed. If it is severely fouled with old grease, dirt and dried oil, it is probably as well to soak it. A small baking tin can be used, or a metal foil dish can be constructed, sufficiently deep to hold just enough paraffin, with a touch of lubricating oil, to cover the lock. The lock should be left totally immersed for a day or two and at the end of the period it can be removed, shaken and dried.

Next the mainspring can be removed; the cock should be brought to the half cock position and the mainspring gripped using either a spring clamp or a pair of grips which may be locked in position. The mainspring is gripped in the half cock position, and the cock is then moved to disengage it from the mainspring which can now be removed. The cock is separated from the tumbler simply by removing the screw; the frizzen spring should be compressed in much the same way as the mainspring and the securing screw removed. The pan cover can also be taken off by the removal of one screw. The rest of the stripping of the lock is fairly simple; the trigger return spring does not really require very much compression as it is quite weak, and the whole mechanism can be stripped down to its component parts.

Cleaning is a matter of personal choice. There are some collectors who prefer to remove only the superficial dirt, leaving the patina and slight pitting of the surface untouched. Others like to polish the metal and bring it back to its original mirror finish. The choice is entirely the collector's. Most collectors prefer to clean the metal, but it is important to remember that all polishing removes some of the metal, and if engraving is present and it is very faint, some thought should be given to just how much would be removed by abrasives. The procedure for polishing must depend upon the degree of rust, but in general a good brushing with a stiff wire brush is the first requirement. If there is any blue or browning on the metal it must again be stressed that any abrasive, no matter how fine, will remove it. It is an unfortunate decision that has to be taken on occasions, but in order to prevent further rusting original colouring may have

to be removed. After the first coarse brushing, steel wool can be used and, if further polishing is thought to be necessary, one of the best materials is that known as jewellers' emery. These are very fine-grade papers which range from a very fine emery down to one which is so fine as to feel like ordinary paper; this last one will give a near mirror-like finish. If there are traces of engraving, browning or blueing which will be removed by the polishing, a record of them should be made before starting work. In order to get even pressure during the polishing it is often worth wrapping the emery around a small block of wood which can be used as a sort of sanding device. For the pan, around the frizzen and other awkward places the emery can be wrapped around the matchsticks in order to reach the rather more inaccessible corners.

Whilst the lock is stripped down it should be examined for any markings: quite often the makers identified the various pieces by Roman numerals or letters, or there may be an initial scratched inside. A note should be taken of all these details. It is also worth considering whether one should place one's own mark on the inside of the lockplate: in these days of so many robberies of antiques it can prove difficult to identify a piece with certainty should it be recovered; however, if some sort of unobtrusive mark is used where it is not readily apparent, this can be used as proof of ownership. This mark does not need to be anything more than initials scratched on the inside of the lockplate. After the parts have all been cleaned, the lock can be reassembled starting with the action and finishing with the mainspring which is slotted into place under tension and then gently released from the clamp.

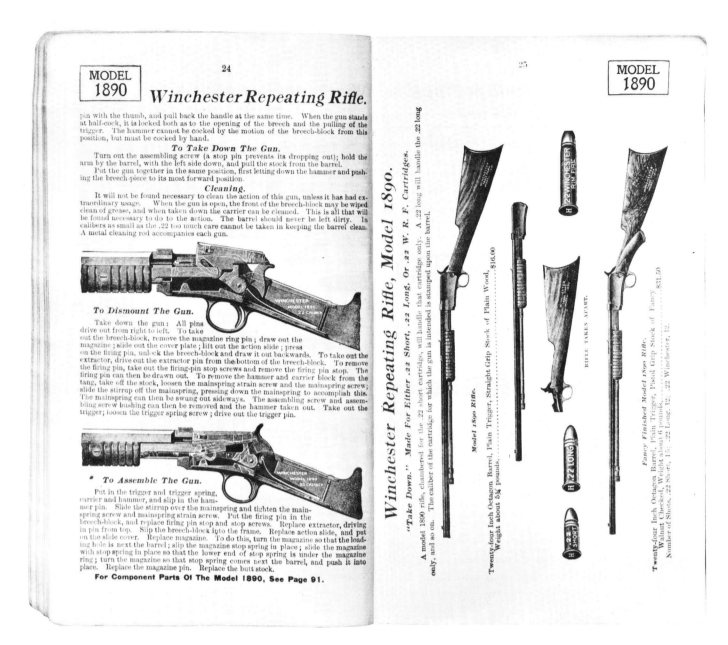

The barrel should be treated in much the same way as the lockplate, but its removal can present more serious problems. On the earlier weapons the barrel is secured to the stock by the pin and lug system, and the pins may become welded into the wood by rust. Tapping them out can be fraught with danger: the stock may be splintered or cracked. If there is any doubt seek professional advice or leave the barrel in place—not a very satisfactory situation but preferable to damaging the stock. The tang screw must also be removed; again this can prove difficult and, if found to be intractable, is another reason for leaving the barrel *in situ*. The question of browning and blueing applies far more to the barrel, for it is often found that when the barrel is removed from the stock the underneath portion retains its original browning, whilst the unprotected top section has been pitted and rubbed to basic metal. It is possible to rebrown metal, and the effect can be almost as good as the original. Some of the books listed below (page 93) give full details of the browning process, and the collector may well be inclined to try it himself. Basically the effect is one of controlled rusting; the browning solution is painted on to the barrel and left to form rust, which is then removed and another coating applied. The process is repeated until just the right patina has developed, when the metal is washed and polished. It is most important before starting the browning to ensure that the surface is thoroughly cleansed of grease and is perfectly smooth. Before cleaning the barrel check it for any markings such as proof marks. Every barrel had to be tested (proved), and this meant that they were examined for visible flaws, then subjected to an excessive charge and examined again. If no fracture or weakness was apparent the barrel was passed, and the fact was indicated by stamping the barrel. A list of these proof marks will be found in some of the books mentioned below. These marks should be recorded, as well as any inscription on the barrel giving a maker's name and address.

The rest of the metal furniture is likely to be of brass or steel and held in place by pins in the same way as the barrel, and therefore the same remarks apply. Again each piece should be checked for any marks.

The stock probably requires least attention. It is

95 Double page from a Winchester catalogue of 1911. Many of these earlier catalogues have been reprinted for the benefit of enthusiasts, for they contain much interesting information. J. B. Bell collection.

96 Percussion pistol converted from flintlock, shown dismantled. *top* Lock internal mechanism, identical with that of a flintlock, and the barrel showing the tang and bracket for sliding bar. *centre* Stock with trigger guard in place. *right* Sliding bar and ramrod. *bottom* Sideplate and screws.

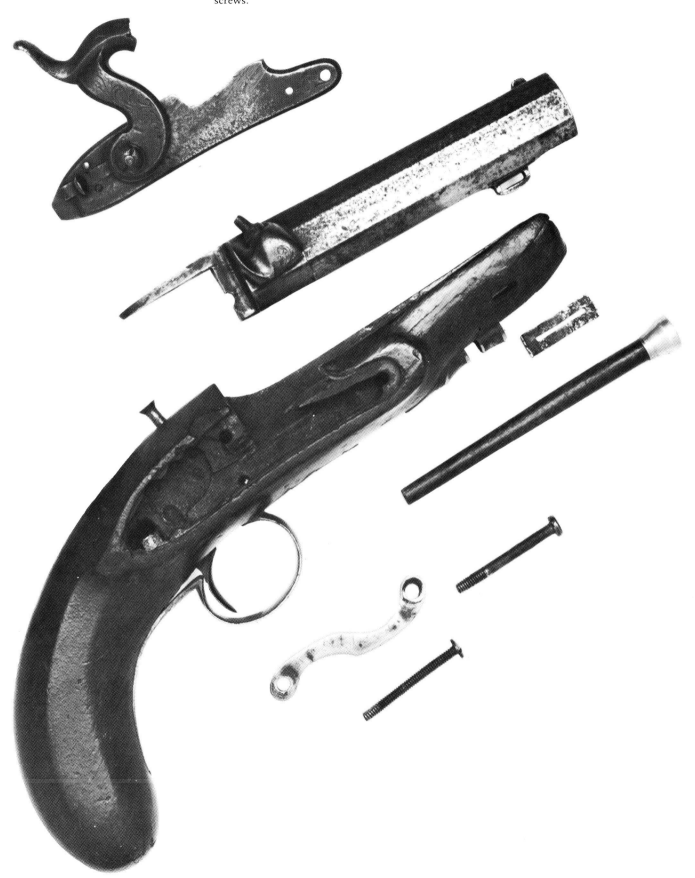

possible to remove some of the worst dents by steaming them. A damp cloth is placed over the dent and a very hot iron applied; the steam enters into the woodwork and literally forces out the fibres to fill up the dent. It is probably as well to practise on another piece of wood before tackling the genuine stock. The woodwork should be thoroughly examined, not only for breaks and cracks, but also for any marks, since many British military weapons will be found to carry various ord-nance marks. Cleaning the woodwork is a matter of preference: there are some who would do no more than give it a thorough wash, whilst others would remove all old stain and varnish, although this tends to give it a slightly new, sanded appearance. In general, unless there are special circumstances, a good wash with reasonably strong detergent and a thorough dry should be sufficient. If the wood is then treated with a good wax polish the effect is quite pleasing.

The whole process is basically the same for percussion weapons as for flintlocks, but with revolvers the strip-ping process is obviously more complicated and should only be undertaken with great care. The various mechanical systems differ, and before attempting to strip any revolver reference should be made to the appropriate books listed below. Most percussion revol-vers were blued, and today there are on the market a number of preparations known as cold blues. The original blueing was achieved by heating the metal in a mixture of leather and bone or in a bath of molten lead. The in-stant blues are just wiped on and are very good indeed; but the majority of them tend to give a duller darker blue than the original, and here again is a decision for the collector. If the revolver has only traces of the original blueing, should one remove all traces of blue and end up with a bright steel pistol, or attempt to replace the blue? Before deciding it is as well to test the blue on a part of the framework which is normally covered, so that if it is unsuccessful the result is not apparent.

Any repairs will obviously be undertaken at this stage, and these days it is certainly easy to obtain spare parts. Several firms produce catalogues which offer hammers and cocks, springs, metal furniture, ramrods and indeed every part needed to repair almost every form of weapon. There are also specialist makers who can reproduce any part which is non-standard. Once again the question is how much restoration one is prepared to accept. There is no right or wrong approach except to say that, broadly speaking, the more restora-tion the less valuable the piece.

Once the weapon has been thoroughly stripped, cleaned and repaired, then a catalogue entry should be made. Again the method of recording is a matter of choice: some collectors like to use a book, whilst others prefer cards. Whichever system is used it is worth considering the question of photographing each item, both for identification in the event of a theft and also for ensuring a complete record in the catalogue of the collection. A standard method of recording is advisable, but obviously the amount of detail included will be a matter for each collector to decide. The following entry is offered merely as a suggested format and is capable of extension and contraction.

Item in collection:	Z6 15
Type of weapon:	Flintlock pocket pistol
Date:	Circa 1780
Maker's name:	Twigg
Furniture:	Brass
Stock:	Walnut, slab sided
Engraving:	Military trophy on side, name on breech
Inscriptions:	None
Overall length:	5 inches
Barrel length:	3 inches
Bore:	.36 inch
Number:	—
Acquired	25.1.71 Sotheby's
Price:	£—
Value:	£—

Price and value can be entered in open figures or, if it is preferred to keep this matter private, in some form of simple coding. A code word can be used as the base, each letter representing a figure.

0	1	2	3	4	5	6	7	8	9
G	U	N	P	O	W	D	E	R	S

Thus £50 becomes £WG, and by this simple means this knowledge is restricted entirely to the collector. It should be remembered that rising prices and inflation alter the value each year, and this figure should be revised annually. It is strongly recommended that insurance should be taken out to cover the value of the collection.

The card could also carry information about the maker and action and may involve some research, albeit very elementary. The flood of literature dealing with the subject of firearms is huge and continues to increase annually. It is therefore extremely difficult for the collector to keep abreast of these new books, but there are a number which can be considered as a basic library. It is not suggested that others are not equally worthy of inclusion, but the titles listed below will offer the average collector a reasonably good source of general information and, since a number of them include exten-sive bibliographies, further research can be undertaken. Quite apart from this secondary research using printed material, there is always the possibility of some original research, particularly in the case of provincial makers, when local rate books, trade directories, newspapers and similar primary sources can often supply some background information.

Bibliography

Books

Antique Firearms (F. Wilkinson) London 1969

Art of the Gunmaker, The (J. Hayward) London, volume I 1965, volume II 1963

Book of Colt Firearms (R. Q. Sutherland and R. L. Wilson) Kansas City 1971

The Book of Pistols and Revolvers (W. H. B. and J. E. Smith) Harrisburg (Pennsylvania) and London 1972

The Book of Rifles (W. H. B. Smith) Harrisburg (Pennsylvania) and London 1972

British Military Firearms 1650–1850 (H. L. Blackmore) London 1961

British Soldier's Firearms, The 1850–1864 (C. H. Roads) London 1964

European and American Arms 1100–1850 (C. Blair) 1962

German Pistols and Revolvers 1871–1945 (I. V. Hogg) London 1971

Guns (F. Wilkinson) London 1970

Guns and Rifles of the World (H. L. Blackmore) London 1965

The Hand Gun (G. Boothroyd) London 1970

Pistols of the World (C. Blair) London 1968

Revolver, The 1818–1865 (A. Taylerson, R. Andrews and J. Frith) London 1968

Revolver, The 1865–1888 (A. Taylerson) London 1966

Revolver, The 1889–1914 (A. Taylerson) London 1970

Revolving Arms (A. Taylerson) London 1967

Small Arms (F. Wilkinson) London 1965

Small Arms Makers (R. Gardiner) London 1953

Periodicals

American Rifleman (Washington, D.C.)

Canadian Journal of Arms Collecting (Mount Royal, Canada)

Gun Digest (Northfield, Illinois)

Gun Report (Aledo, Illinois)

Guns Illustrated (Chicago, Illinois)

Guns Review (Harrogate, Yorkshire)

Acknowledgments

The Publishers would like to thank the owners of the pieces reproduced in this book for kindly making them available for photography.

All photographs were taken by Paul Forrester of Michael Dyer Associates with the exception of the following: Plates 6, 9, 10, 35, 67, 68, 70, 73, 74, 75, which were supplied by Sotheby & Co.; Plates 55, 57, which were supplied by Elliott & Snowdon; Plate 62, which was supplied by Holland & Holland. Plate 58 is reproduced by kind permission of the Trustees of the National Gallery, London.

Index

The numbers in bold type refer to illustrations